How to Win in Spiritual Warfare

by Joseph E. Smith

About the Author

For twelve years, Joe held various lay positions in Southern Baptist churches. In 1971, he became frustrated at the lack of real spiritual growth, even though he was involved in many activities. His search for the missing ingredient led him into a full awareness of the ministry of the Holy Spirit and the victorious life He gives.

In 1972, Joe began to be used by the Holy Spirit in youth revivals and other evangelical crusades. This brought him in contact with Maranatha Ministries and, in 1974, he became associated with Maranatha, establishing churches on university campuses around the world. In 1978, he left a seventeen year career in the chemical industry (he has a degree in organic chemistry) to devote all his time to Christian work.

Joe is recognized as a prophet in the body of Christ and with his wife has traveled extensively throughout the world, ministering on campuses, various churches, conferences, and radio and television. They have two grown sons; one is a pastor and other is attending the University of Kentucky.

Acknowledgment

I wish to express my deepest appreciation to Andy and Peggy Anderson, Anderson Advertising Art, Denver, Colorado, for the art work, layout and typesetting; they also encouraged me to continue my labors to complete this work. My thanks also to the several people who reviewed the manuscript and made helpful suggestions.

Dedication:

To my wife, sweetheart, and friend, Katie, who has shared in my victories and defeats, constantly encouraging me to press on.

J.E.S.

Scriptures marked NAS quoted from the New American Standard Bible by Lockman Foundation, 1960, 1962, 1963, 1968, 1971, 1972, 1973, 1975, 1977; all other Scriptures quoted from the King James Version

How to Win in Spiritual Warfare

© 1984 by Joseph E. and Katie M. Smith

ISBN # 0-918923-01-8

Printed in the United States of America.
J & K Books
P.O. Box 16594
Tampa, FL 33687
(813) 986-4292

TABLE OF CONTENTS

Author's Preface

Every Christian has been faced with fear, worry, doubt, depression, rejection, and a host of other techniques the enemy uses as weapons to overcome and rob them of the abundant life promised by God in Christ Jesus.

Many times the enemy has been successful in waging war against Christians because they did not know their authority and how to use it. Although the scriptures do not teach specific methods and techniques with regard to how believers can use their authority in Christ, they *do* reveal concepts and principles.

One area of spiritual warfare in which one can buy numerous books and tapes is deliverance and inner healing. Reflecting the need to be freed from the oppression of Satan, these books and tapes present methods of obtaining freedom from various oppressions. As everyone who has received this type of ministry knows, being set free and remaining free are two different subjects.

These Bible studies will not discuss deliverance and inner healing as such. But they will discuss *principles and concepts* for developing our authority as believers and using it to remain free. We will also discuss *how to avoid the snares* of the enemy. The Bible says that Jesus has provided for every Christian total victory over every power of the enemy: "Behold, I have given you authority to tread upon serpents and scorpions, and over all the power of the enemy, and nothing shall injure you" (Luke 10:19, NAS). In studying these concepts and principles, believers should become aware of their *weapons of warfare* and how to use them. In so doing, they will become effective soldiers in God's army, who can successfully wage war against the enemy and win triumphantly!

It would be too vast an undertaking to list every weapon of warfare used by the enemy and how we can win over each one of them. For sake of manageability, those we do discuss will be grouped under major headings. This gives you, the reader, an opportunity to expand the list or even transfer from one list to another if you so desire. For each group, principles and concepts on how to successfully wage war and win triumphantly are studied.

Keep in mind as you do these studies that just as a recruit in the U.S. Army must be taught and trained to develop his skills in using various weapons of war, so it is with you. For example, the first time a recruit fires his rifle, he may miss the whole target even though he was aiming for a bulls eye.

In like manner, you may not experience total victory in your first attempt to successfully wage war against fear or some other weapon of the enemy. However, as you practice using the weapon God has given to overcome every power of the enemy, you will find yourself becoming more and more proficient in using them, until you are able to successfully wage war and win triumphantly over *all* the weapons of the enemy.

In the book of Galatians we are told of the nine fruit of the Holy Spirit which are available to each believer: "love, joy, peace, long-suffering, gentleness, goodness, faithfulness, meekness, and self-control; against such things there is no law." (Galatians 5:22) These nine fruit can be developed into *nine specific weapons* in our warfare against the enemy.

The following chart lists love, joy, and peace in the first column, how we learn to use them in the second column, and the major areas of warfare in the 3rd column. The last column indicates the victory which will be wrought in the overcomer's life, using these fruit of the Spirit as weapons. Each area will be discussed and expanded upon in specific chapters to provide the principles and concepts involved in each war.

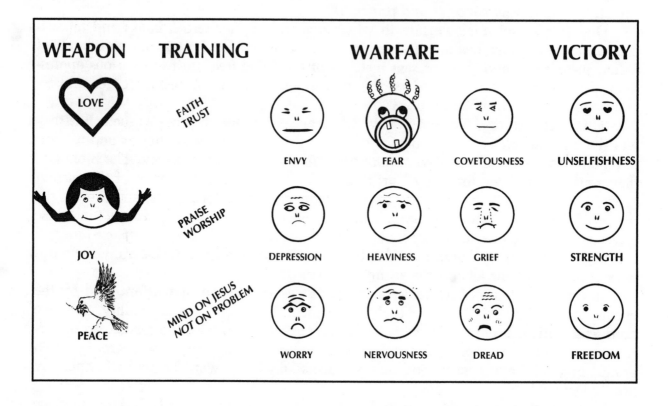

Subsequent studies in Volumes II and III will detail the remaining fruit and how they may be applied as weapons in our war against the enemy, so that ultimately you will be able to utilize all nine fruit of the Spirit skillfully, effectively, and victoriously!

CHAPTER ONE: HOW THE WAR BEGAN AND ENDED

The First Battle

Spiritual warfare on earth began in the garden of Eden with a man and woman named Adam and Eve. They had been placed in the garden by God, their Creator, to cultivate it and keep it. In time, they discovered that God had an adversary called Satan, who desired that they serve him rather than the One True God who created them. They also discovered that Satan's tactics and methods of warfare involved immoral and unethical tactics—he goes by the rule that all is fair in war. They learned this lesson through Satan speaking to Eve about eating of the fruit of the tree of the knowledge of good and evil. This was the only tree in the garden that God had forbidden them to eat of its fruit. Satan had no qualms or misgivings about seducing Eve into believing that God had lied to her and Adam about the consequences of eating the fruit from the tree of the knowledge of good and evil. He suggested that God had a good reason for lying: if they ate of the fruit, their eyes would be opened and they would be as God. Many sermons have been preached on how Eve was snared by this lie and accusation of the enemy, disobeyed God by taking of the forbidden fruit, and gave some to Adam who also ate of it. The ending to this story is familiar to many: they met the enemy, they waged war ineffectively, they lost.

God's Answer to the Fall of Man

After the fall of Adam and Eve, it appeared Satan had won in his war to have man serve him rather than God. But this was not to be the end. Although he had indeed won a major victory, the war was by no means over. However, this did present a seemingly impossible situation for God. How could He deal righteously and justly with both Adam and Satan and still maintain His integrity? God is love. Therefore, He could not repay evil with evil, but must return good for evil. On the other hand, the power, dominion, and authority of Satan over man must be broken. Had Satan also snared God?

No!

God had a solution which He revealed to man and Satan in Genesis 3:15, where God said, "I am going to bring forth a seed from the woman which will break Satan's lordship over man."

1. From the following scriptures determine specifically how this *seed* was to come and what His name was to be:
   a. Genesis 12:3 _____
   b. Genesis 49:10 _____
   c. Psalm 89:3–4 _____

d. Isaiah 7:14 _____

e. Luke 1:31 _____

Therefore, in the fullness of time, God brought forth a seed of woman which was conceived by the Holy Spirit. His name was Jesus. He was like the first Adam before Adam sinned. He was not under the authority of Satan, but under the authority of God.

Satan's War Against Jesus

Consequently, Satan launched all-out war against Jesus, designed to snare Him as he had the first Adam:

2. By reading each of the following scriptures define Satan's method of attack:

    a. Matthew 27:29 _____

    b. Matthew 27:39 _____

    c. Acts 8:33 _____

    d. Matthew 9:11 _____

    e. Matthew 11:19 _____

    f. Matthew 26:65 _____

    g. Mark 3:21 _____

    h. John 7:20 _____

    i. John 10:20 _____

    j. John 9:16 _____

    k. Hebrews 4:15 _____

    l. Matthew 13:57 _____

    m. Luke 4:29 _____

    n. John 1:11 _____

    o. Luke 16:14 _____

    p. Matthew 4:8–10 _____

    q. Matthew 27:22–23 _____

Since none of these efforts to snare Jesus worked, there appeared to be only one course of action left open to Satan by which to gain control over this second Adam, Jesus. He must exercise his power of death. He had used this power of physical death down through the years to overcome men of God, especially the prophets. In so doing, Satan had kept them from turning the hearts of people back to God.

3. What instruments did Satan use to kill the prophets?

    a. I Kings 18:13 _____

    b. Nehemiah 9:24–26 _____

    c. Matthew 23:29–35 _____

    d. Matthew 23:37 _____

4. How did Satan wage war to bring death upon Jesus?

    a. Acts 13:23–30 _____

    b. Matthew 27:35 _____

Satan proceeded to implement his plan against Jesus by arousing the religious leaders' hatred for Him to the point that they desired to see Him dead. Then he directed the trial of Jesus, and during the trial gave Jesus plenty of opportunities to be snared and overcome. In his final act of war, he had Jesus mocked, beaten, spit upon, reviled and, finally, nailed naked to a cross. Yet, even while hanging on the cross, Jesus cried out, "Father forgive them (the people) for they know not what they do" (Luke 23:34).

5. Did Jesus ever sin?
   Hebrews 4:15 _____

6. What are the consequences (or wages) of sin?
   Romans 6:23 _____
   Hanging on the cross at Calvary, Jesus at last cried out, "It is finished."

7. What did He do next?
   Luke 23:46 _____
   _____

How Jesus Won the War

Jesus healed every sickness and disease which Satan put upon man: He released men from unclean spirits; Demons trembled and obeyed His commands; He exercised authority and dominion over the natural elements; He spoke and the wind ceased to blow and ocean winds became still; He was in complete dominion and authority over all creation, including Satan. The following scripture reveals His complete dominion and authority:

> And when evening had come, they brought to Him many who were demon-possessed; and He cast out the spirits with a word, and healed all who were ill in order that what was spoken through Isaiah the prophet might be fulfilled, saying, "He Himself took our infirmities, and carried away our diseases." . . . , And the men marveled, saying, "What kind of man is this, that even the winds and the sea obey Him?" (Matthew 8:16–17, 27, NAS).

Even in death, Jesus was victorious, for He could commend His own spirit unto God, even though Satan was the one with the power and authority of death. It had not yet dawned upon Satan that the wages of sin are death, and Jesus had not sinned! Therefore, Jesus did not have to die. Death had no power over Him. But Jesus allowed this to take place because He loved us and wanted us to be free from the authority, dominion, and lordship of Satan. He died for sins that we might live.

8. Why does the thief, Satan, come, and why did Jesus come?
   John 10:10
   a. _____
   b. _____
   c. _____
   d. _____

9. What will a good shepherd do for his sheep?
   John 10:11 _____

10. Who gave Jesus the authority to lay down His life?
    John 10:17–18 _____

11. In giving up His life, what was Jesus accomplishing?
    a. John 15:13 _____
    b. I John 3:16 _____
    c. Romans 5:6–8 _____
    d. Hebrews 2:14–15 _____

e. Acts 4:8–12 _____

f. Romans 10:9 _____

As we have shown above, in crucifying Jesus Satan committed an illegal act, and God was now free to use this as a means of freeing man from Satan's lordship. God could accept the illegal death of Jesus as payment in full for every man's sin.

How the War Continues Today

God has now won the war. Jesus met the enemy, waged successful warfare, and won. Victory is His. Satan is defeated! (Read Colossians 2:15). However, the battle continues on as Satan now wars to keep his subjects—men and women—from accepting the victory Jesus won for them at Calvary. He attempts to blind their minds and keep them from turning to God through the Lord Jesus Christ. He uses several methods to accomplish this, which may be summed up as follows:

1. **Inducing doubt** as to who Jesus really is—introducing all manner of deception by declaring Jesus to be anyone but the Son of God and Redeemer of man.
2. **Creating a negative impression** of God as a God of wrath and judgment, rather than love; this blinds people to God's love and Father nature as revealed in the life and death of Jesus.
3. **Encouraging skepticism** as to the reality of God, thus leading to the worship of things created rather than to worship of the Creator.
4. **Teaching through humanism** that man is capable of being his own god and solving his own problems, using human means and understandings.
5. **Obtaining belief** that a certain state of moral excellence must be obtained before coming to God.
6. **Creating the fearful impression** that the cost of turning to God is too high by claiming there are too many desires and pleasures of life which one must hold onto for fulfillment.
7. **Instilling fear** that one cannot really live the Christian life.

How You Can Begin to Win the War

Turning to God requires an intelligent decision with regard to whom we will serve. No one can serve two masters; no one can live as a citizen in both the kingdom of darkness and the kingdom of light. The decision to renounce and break all ties with Satan's kingdom and embrace Jesus as Lord is a love decision. It constitutes loving God for who He is, our Creator, not for what He can do. It consists of accepting His love which He demonstrated in the life of Jesus. It involves recognizing Jesus as Lord and accepting His way as the way for living in every area of life. It instills a desire to serve Him, love Him, and obey Him with all our heart, soul, mind, and strength because He alone is worthy of all love and devotion. Turning to God also means a decision to enter into **the warfare of establishing the kingdom of God in our own lives and the lives of our loved ones and friends,** thus destroying the works of Satan here on earth. Furthermore, a decision to acknowledge Jesus as Lord gives us the full assurance of victory in overcoming every weapon the enemy has raised up to exalt himself at our expense.

4

If you have never made a decision to totally commit your life to Jesus as loving Lord and Master, why not stop right here and do so. That's called repentance. Next, tell the Father of your decision through the following prayer, or one similar to it. Prayer is simply talking to God:

> Father, I ask in the name of Jesus that you forgive my sins, and cleanse me of all wrong doings. I turn from ruling my own life. Instead, I acknowledge Jesus as Lord of my life, and from this time onward will choose Him and His ways as my standard for living. I now open my heart and invite Jesus to take control of my life. Thank you for receiving me, forgiving me, cleansing me, and making me the kind of person you created me to be. Amen.

How You Continue to Win

Finally, whenever someone makes the decision to accept the Lordship of Jesus, they have already waged war and overcome the first obstacle toward victory. They have also stopped believing Satan's lies about God. But, they have not stopped Satan from using other lies and tactics to prevent further progress. He will now attempt to keep the believer from experiencing the abundant life in Christ. He will also try to prevent him from serving God. According to Romans 7:23 and II Corinthians 10:3–6, **the battlefield is the mind.** Although the human spirit has been recreated and made alive with God now dwelling therein, the soul has not been recreated. Therefore, the Holy Spirit encourages many times in the scriptures the renewing of the mind and getting knowledge through the Word of God. As God's subjects we must *now learn to think and act differently.* This is accomplished through yielding our reasoning and thinking to the Christ who now lives right inside of us.

12. What is the believer to put off and to put on?
    Ephesians 4:22,24
    a. v. 22 _____
    b. v. 24 _____
13. What area is to be renewed?
    a. Ephesians 4:23 _____
    b. Romans 12:2 _____
14. What else must the mind increase in to be renewed?
    Colossians 1:10 _____

The **true knowledge of truth** becomes **the first essential weapon of warfare** and must be diligently sought with the earnest and sincere desire to obey all revealed truth.

There is only one source of truth—God's Word. John 1:1,14 reveals Jesus as being the Word of God made flesh; therefore, whenever we know truth (i.e. Jesus), we are **set free** and **kept free** from the oppression of the enemy. As it is written in John 8:36, "If therefore the Son shall make you free, you shall be free indeed."

Equally radical truth concerning self must be accepted as revealed by the scriptures, not by any biased, colored, or diluted understanding. Deliverance from believing lies and being deceived is accomplished through believing truth. This begins with the salvation experience when the sinner **believes the truth with regard to himself and Jesus.** Just as the enemy waged war to keep the sinner from believing this truth, he will now wage war in an attempt to keep the believer from believing other truths regarding himself and Jesus.

Basically, the tactic involves keeping the believer from the full realization that God now lives in him and does not exist as some mystical spirit someplace "out there". Our finite minds cannot fully understand that through Christ Jesus we have been **united with Deity**. It is no longer a matter of trying to get to God, or find God, or be with God, because *He now lives in us*. This realization caused the apostle Paul to exclaim, "Christ in you the hope of glory!" (Colossians 1:27). It made the apostle John declare, "Greater is He that is in you than he that is in the world." (I John 4:4)

The Result of Victory

Therefore, it is now a matter of learning how to *release* the knowledge, wisdom, love, and all other attributes of God from the now recreated spirit *into* the soul. This will occur naturally as we deepen our intimate, personal relationship with Jesus through prayer, Bible study, worship, praise, and ministering unto Him. As we do this, we are being changed from an earthly image into the image of Jesus.

15. What image has God determined a believer to be conformed into?
    Romans 8:29 _____

Therefore, it is a lie to believe that one must reflect the image of darkness rather than the image of Jesus. It is a subtle way of saying the devil has more power than God.

Therefore, let no one be deceived any longer by the fact that they are not totally in the image of Christ. This does not make God a liar, but reveals the *work which is still to be accomplished in each of us*. It should be noted here that each Christian does have areas of victory in their lives that are Christ-like. But each Christian also has areas of life that need to be transformed and become Christ-like. This is not to give the illusion that it will happen overnight. Nevertheless, one day this earth is going to be filled with victorious overcomers in the image of Jesus. For we have this hope that "we shall be like Him". (I John 3:2)

16. What does this hope cause to happen in the life of a believer?
    I John 3:1–3 _____

Although the enemy may hinder and stall the believer's progress in some areas, he can not prevent God's Word from being fulfilled. In II Peter 1:3–4 (NAS), we read these glorious promises:

> Seeing that His divine power has granted to us *everything* pertaining to life and godliness, through the true knowledge of Him who called us by His own glory and excellence. For by these He has granted to us His precious and magnificent promises, in order that by them you might become partakers of the divine nature, having escaped the corruption that is in the world by lust.

These promises are found in God's Word.

How to Develop Spiritually

In the following studies, principles and concepts from God's Word will be used to reveal **how you may develop spiritually** and **how you may use your spiritual weapons to wage war successfully against the enemy** in order to live in total victory through Christ Jesus.

Keep in mind that we are not waging war against flesh and blood. It is *not* a natural or physical battle we are in, but spiritual. Therefore, our weapons and means of warfare must be **learned in the spirit and brought over into the mind;** otherwise, we will find ourselves attempting to fight a spiritual battle with weapons of flesh and blood which will not produce victory. But when we apply the mighty weapons of God, which are spiritual, we discover we can pull down strongholds, cast out vain imaginations, and take captive every thought which exalts itself and bring it into the obedience of the knowledge of Christ Jesus. (II Corinthians 10:3–5)

Questions to Stimulate Thought and Revelation from the Lord

17. Who is God's and every Christian's adversary? _____
18. Who were the first ones involved in spiritual warfare? _____
_____
19. Did they win or lose? _____ Why? _____
_____
20. Whom did God send to war against Satan? _____
21. Did He win or lose? _____ Why? _____
_____
22. How does Satan attempt to keep his subjects from turning to Jesus? _____
23. What does turning to Jesus involve? _____
_____
24. Can a Christian win over Satan in every spiritual battle? _____
25. What are the Christian's weapons of warfare, and how are they developed? _____
_____
_____

We now turn to the first three fruit of the Spirit to show how they can be used as weapons to win in spiritual warfare.

Answers to Questions

1. a. Through the seed of Abraham
   b. Of the tribe of Judah
   c. Descendant of King David and his throne
   d. Born of a virgin
   e. His name is Jesus

2. a. Mocked by men
   b. Verbal abuse by men
   c. Humiliation
   d. Accusation by Pharisees of keeping wrong company
   e. Accusation by men of being a glutton and a drunk
   f. Accusation by High Priest of blasphemy
   g. Accusation by own people of insanity
   h. Accusation by the multitude of having a demon
   i. Accusation of treason
   j. Accusation by Pharisees of breaking the Sabbath
   k. Tempted in every way possible, as *we* are
   l. Dishonored
   m. Threats of violence and murder
   n. Rejection
   o. Scoffed at and ridiculed
   p. Offer of the kingdoms of this world to worship Satan
   q. Crowd demands for His crucifixion

3. a. Jezebel—a queen or woman in authority
   b. People who entered the promised land
   c. Religious leaders, hypocrites
   d. Jerusalem, the capital city

4. a. Stirred up religious leaders to condemn Him
   b. Crucifixion

5. No

6. Death

7. He then commended His spirit to depart from His body into the hands of God

8. a. steal
   b. kill
   c. destroy
   d. give abundant life

9. Lay down His life

10. Himself as received from God the Father

11. a. Demonstrating true love
    b. Teaching us God's love
    c. Obeying God's command of love

d. Rendered devil powerless
e. Salvation for men through His Name
f. Salvation through confession with mouth and belief with heart that God raised Jesus from the dead

12. a. Lay aside old self
    b. Put on the new self

13. The mind

14. Our knowledge of God

15. The image of His Son

16. That we be purified just as He is pure

17. Satan

18. Adam and Eve

19. Lose. They did not understand spiritual warfare and ended up believing the lies and sinned, choosing Satan over God.

20. Jesus

21. Win. He knew how to wage war against Satan. He believed the Father at all times, being prepared by knowing Him and the Word.

22. Doubt, lies, skepticism, humanism, false pictures of God

23. Making a love decision to acknowledge Him as Lord, turning from self and sin (repentance)

24. Yes

25. The nine fruit of the Spirit. By believing the truth about Jesus and our own self and by releasing Him who is in our recreated spirit into our soul, we thereby learn in our spirit truth to bring over to our mind.

CHAPTER TWO: LOVE

What is Love?

> And now abideth faith, hope, love, these three; but the greatest of these is love. (I Corinthians 13:13)

> A new commandment I give unto you, that ye love one another as I have loved you, that ye also love one another. By this all men will know that ye are my disciples, if you have love one for another. (John 13:34–35)

In order to see how love can be used as a weapon to win in spiritual warfare, we need to understand what love really is and what Jesus said about it. Jesus told His disciples that all men would know they were of Him if they had love for one another. He qualified this love by saying, "As I have loved you."

1. If one does not love, what is he revealing about himself?
    I John 4:8 _____
2. How do we know we have passed from death unto life?
    I John 3:14 _____

The supreme test of a believer is not with regard to his church membership, baptism, confirmation, church attendance, Bible study, witnessing, or any such thing. The supreme test is whether or not he **loves as God loves.**

I became aware of this through a Bible study on I John. Verse after verse expressed the theme of love and stated if one did not love, he did not know God. These statements presented a problem for me, because I knew some people in my congregation that I did not even like, let alone love. It was obvious that I must learn to love in obedience to what God has commanded. Although I did not see how I could possibly love in this way, I willingly submitted the problem to God. I told Him I wanted His love to flow unchecked in my life and that I was willing to change. I had no idea this decision would turn out to be the key which would unlock the door to abundant living for me.

Because love is the foundation for all Christian action, it is necessary to have a Biblical understanding of the word "love" as expressed in the Greek language of the New Testament. Otherwise, the commandment to love will appear to be an impossibility.

Most people are familiar with love only as it is conceived by the world. This was true in Jesus' day also. The common Greek words used during this time were *stergo, phileo,* and *eros*. "Stergo" expressed the love of husband and wife, brother and sister, parent and child. "Phileo" expressed the love between friends or "brotherly love". Another Greek word used was "Eros", which referred to the sensual, including sexual acts. Today, our society constantly claims that love is sex. This type of love is expressed in most songs, books, movies, and television shows. However, this common, human love constitutes both a blessing and a curse. While it may seem to create some very beautiful relationships, it most often destroys relationships. It brings one out of every two marriages to the divorce courts and is the cause of untold human suffering and agony, being the parent of most tears and sorrows.

Furthermore, "Eros" love by itself is purely selfish, and feeds upon self-gratification, the highest form of self-gratification being sex. Consequently, it is not surprising to find this concept of love being widely promoted. Advertising leads men and women to believe that the use of almost anything creates sex appeal which makes them "with it". Even eye glasses and toothpaste are advertised for their sex appeal.

It was not too different in the time Jesus lived here on earth. Therefore, Jesus was faced with the problem of expressing a love for which there was no concept. He was establishing in the world a Divine Love, the true, pure love that had been displaced in man's heart by selfishness. Therefore, when He spoke to His disciples concerning the new law which would govern His Kingdom, He created a new concept for "agape".

> A new commandment I give unto you, that ye love (agape) one another even as I have loved you, that ye also love (agape) one another. By this all men will know that ye are my disciples, if you have love (agape) for one another. John 13:34–35

The disciples did not understand agape until Pentecost.

> And the multitude of them that believed were of one heart and of one soul: neither said any of them that aught of the things which he possessed was his own; but they had all things in common. And with great power gave the apostles witness of the resurrection of the Lord Jesus: and great grace was upon them all. Neither was there any among them that lacked: for as many as were possessors of lands or houses sold them, and brought the prices of the things that were sold, and laid them down at the apostles' feet: and distribution was made unto every man according as he had need. Acts 4:32–35

This is a description of *agape in action*. It demonstrated to the Jews in Jerusalem *a new way of living and acting*. This was a new form of love that sought not its own. It was a love which showed the nature of God rather than the nature of man. It was radically different from human love which existed in the old, unregenerated man. Because these believers had been born again, their nature had been recreated and a new creation having God's nature had appeared.

The True Characteristic of a Christian

The one, true mark of being born again is the manifestation of agape. Although other marks of being a Christian can be copied, agape cannot be duplicated or copied. No one can love as God loves unless he has received God, for God is love.

3. What is the greatest form of love?
   John 15:13 _____

4. How do we know love?
   I John 3:16 _____

5. What ought we do?
   I John 3:16 _____

Agape-love is the missing ingredient which robs many Christians of the blessings from serving God. If one is serving as a pastor, teacher, musician, or in any other service from a sense of duty or obligation rather than love, the Scriptures declare it will not profit him. For anyone to accomplish God's will, he must be **love inspired** and **love motivated**, for the Scriptures declare:

> If I speak with the tongues of men and of angels, but do not have love, I have become a *noisy* gong or a clanging cymbal. And if I have the gift of prophesy, and know all mysteries, and all knowledge, and if I have all faith, so as to remove mountains, but do not have love, *I am nothing.* And if I give all my possessions to feed the poor, and if I deliver my body to be burned, but do not have love, it *profits me nothing.* (I Corinthians 13:1–3 NAS)

One of the highest prized gifts is to speak eloquently. Many men strive to do so and yet, if one were able to speak oh so beautifully, but did not have agape, he would be as a noisy gong.

This explains why so many churches are empty. It is also one reason for the failure of Christianity to reach out into the world. Men have become clanging cymbals, speaking a lot of empty words. **Because they do not have agape, their words contain no life and do not profit the speaker or the listener.** Suppose someone had the ability to see into the future and accurately tell events that would happen. You would not find a building large enough to hold the crowds. Furthermore, if someone had the ability to explain the great mysteries of our world, how it began, how it operates, he would receive untold acclaim as the greatest teacher to ever live. And if someone had the faith to overcome in every situation, the mountain-moving faith that Christians desire, yet did not have agape, all these would be nothing.

In the same manner, if someone works and labors long hours, gives his very life to help meet the needs of food, medicine, and education for the needy, and has not agape, he has wasted his life. It has profited him nothing.

A Contrast Between Human and Divine Love

The theme of agape as continued in I Corinthians 13:4–7 reveals a *sharp contrast* between Divine love and human love. Let's take a look at what these verses reveal:

6. From verses 4–7 list the characteristics of Divine Love.

    v. 4 a. _____

    b. _____

CONTRAST: Human love may suffer long, because there is no way out of the circumstances. But, it will not stay kind. It grows bitter.

    v. 4 c. _____

    d. _____

    e. _____

CONTRAST: Human love is always arrogant and boastful. It is very jealous of self and those who pay homage to self. It is envious of others. Human love centers on self, and whenever self is removed, human love crumbles since self is its own strength.

    v. 5 f. _____

    g. _____

11

h. _____
i. _____

CONTRAST: Human love is always seeking to elevate self and becomes provoked whenever its efforts are frustrated. It boasts that all is fair in love and war. Human love believes you better do it to the other fellow before he does it to you. To reach its goal of elevating self, human love continually motivates evil and discusses the means to help win, regardless of the cost.

v. 6 j. _____
k. _____

CONTRAST: Human love says, "I may forgive, but I will never forget." Human love always rejoices when the enemy gets what he deserves. It only rejoices over truth when truth elevates and gratifies self.

v. 7 l. _____
m. _____
n. _____
o. _____
v. 8 p. _____

CONTRAST: Human love will only bear the things which promise to reward self. It is not loyal to others, but it is always suspicious of their actions, expecting the worst from them rather than the best.

Agape never fails. Human love is always failing.

Agape is the new love Jesus brought to us and commanded us to be governed by rather than our natural love.

How to Develop Your Love Life

Meanwhile, as God made me aware of the importance of loving as He loves, I began to pray and ask God for love, agape love. But as I prayed for agape love, He told me to quit because I already had agape love. He explained it this way: If someone were to ask you for your coat, you could take it off and give it to him. But, if he asked you for your nature, you would have to give him not only your coat, but everything you have. Because God is love, when I received Christ, I received love—Divine love. Agape is God's nature and therefore, I did not need to pray and ask for something I had *already received*. Instead, I needed to ask *how* His love could become released and revealed in me.

When I asked for this revelation, I was amazed at the simplicity of the answer. *You love by faith* just as you do everything else in the Christian life. For the Christian walks by faith, not sight, according to II Corinthians 5:7. **It is walking by faith and trusting God that we are trained in the use of love as a weapon in spiritual warfare.**

7. What has been poured out in the heart of every believer?
Romans 5:5 _____
8. How is this accomplished? _____

By faith (trust in God's Word) you must believe agape-love is *now within you waiting to be released*. When you accepted Jesus Christ into your spirit you received a new nature, a Divine nature, God's nature. This nature also contains joy, peace, longsuffering, kindness, goodness, faithfulness, gentleness, and self-control.

12

There are those who think God gives to one love, to another peace, to another joy, and so forth. But they are not sure what, if any, of these God has given them. The truth is that God only has *one gift* which He gives to everyone who will accept Him—and that is *Himself through Christ Jesus.*

The difficulty in loving with God's love rather than human love is in *putting off old habits* and *breaking old thought patterns.* This is accomplished one day at a time, by breaking one habit at a time, and being determined to allow God's love to replace your human love. The Living Bible puts it this way:

> But to obtain these gifts, you need more than faith; you must also work hard to be good, and even that is not enough. For then, you must learn to know God better and discover what He wants you to do.

> Next, learn to put aside your own desires so that you will become patient and godly, gladly letting God have His way with you. This will make possible the next step, which is for you to enjoy other people and like them. **And finally, you will grow to love them deeply.**

> The more you go on in this way, the more you will grow strong spiritually and become fruitful and useful to our Lord Jesus Christ. But anyone who fails to go after these additions to faith is blind indeed or at least very shortsighted, and has forgotten that God delivered him from the old life of sin so that now he can live a strong, good life for the Lord.

> So, dear brothers, work hard to prove that you really are among those God has called and chosen, and you will never stumble or fall away. And God will open wide the gates of heaven for you to enter into the eternal kingdom of our Lord and Saviour Jesus Christ.
> II Peter 1:5–11 (The Living Bible)

These scriptures are a beautiful lesson on how to develop love. As God's love replaces our human love, we learn to love all people and begin to see how God works through others to accomplish this in our lives.

How Love Affects Your Relationship With Others

We also learn that God works through people for good; Satan works through people for evil. Many times, in both cases, the person may not be aware of his influence in a given situation. An act or statement can create either good or bad reactions inside you.

An example of Satan using someone, without the person being aware of it, is found in Matthew 16:21–24. Jesus told his disciples he would one day go into Jerusalem and suffer many things. He also told them He would be killed. Peter obviously did not like what he heard and boldly told Jesus this just could not happen. Jesus turned to Peter and said "Get behind Me, Satan! You are a stumbling block to Me: for you are not *setting your mind* on God's interests, but man's" (verse 23, NAS).

Why would Jesus talk to Peter in that manner? Because Jesus knew the source of that statement was Satan who had influenced Peter's mind and caused him to say those words. Knowing this, Jesus did not respond to Peter but to the source.

From this example, it becomes evident that people are never the source of a problem. They may speak and act in such a way that is wrong and upsets you, but the root of their actions is your adversary, Satan.

9. What do we not war against, and what do we war against?

13

Eph. 6:12 a. _____

        b. _____

        _____

In like manner, if we do not separate a person from his deeds, we will war against flesh and blood which is the wrong enemy. In so doing, we will suffer defeat rather than victory.

One way I have discovered of avoiding the snare of responding to people is to focus my attention on *releasing love* to the person involved. This is accomplished by silently asking Jesus to reach out and love the person, letting His love flow through me and out to the one involved. If things are really hot, I ask Jesus to dump an oversized load of love upon them.

Furthermore, it becomes important for us to know that we do not have to be ruled by our emotions and feelings. They are no longer free to do as they please and to make demands on us which are against God's will and His Word. We must therefore purpose in our hearts that our emotions and feelings will be *disciplined* and brought under the authority and lordship of Jesus. They are to act only in the manner prescribed by the Holy Spirit.

As you enter into this battle remember, God has promised you victory if you will not faint or grow weary. Consequently, the only way you can lose is by quitting. You must not believe that sin is so strong and your habits so controlling that they cannot be overcome; otherwise you will quit and give up the fight of faith. It should be noted that freedom from the mastery of sin over us is granted us supernaturally through Jesus becoming sin for us (2 Cor. 5:21).

The Holy Spirit was aware of the battles and the suffering we would experience when He had Paul write in Romans 8:18 (NAS), "For I consider that the sufferings of this present time are not worthy to be compared with the glory that is to be revealed to us."

10. Is sin the master of a believer?

    Rom. 6:14 _____

11. How do we keep sin from being our master?

    Rom. 6:11–13, 17, 19

    6:11 (a) _____

    6:12 (b) _____

    6:13 (c) _____

    6:17 (d) _____

    6:19 (e) _____

Wouldn't it be wonderful to have love so abundantly?! There would be no more strife, envyings, division, hate, jealousy, or resentment—just love—love abundantly!

What Love Does

Love is the force behind everything which is of God. It is not a question of denomination or doctrine, or how well we confess to be a Christian, or how many scriptures we can quote. The question for every act of a Christian is whether or not it is rooted and grounded in love.

According to Galatians 5:6, love is even the force behind faith. And we are further told in Hebrews 11:6 that without faith it is impossible to please God. For these reasons we can never really know and understand spiritual truths or be pleasing to God without love. Although Christ dwells in us by faith and we walk by faith, faith works by love.

Love is not weakness; it is power. *Love* brought God to this earth to dwell as a human being and to die for our sins (John 3:16). *Love* wiped out sickness, diseases, poverty, death, and conquered over every power of the enemy. *Love* also casts out all fear (I John 4:18). For most Christians, these truths have not been realized. Many are afraid of driving, afraid of flying, afraid of the dark, afraid of sickness, afraid of getting old, afraid of dying, afraid of losing their job, afraid of witnessing, afraid of. . . . The list goes on and on. There seems to be no end to the things people are afraid of. However, when we realize that God loves us just as He loved Jesus (John 17:23) we begin to trust Him in every situation; and this faith, working by love, will cast out all fear.

Love in the Home

I used to wonder why the Holy Spirit had Paul write in Ephesians 5:25, "Husbands, love (agape) your wife, even as Christ also loved the church and gave Himself for it." Now I am beginning to see why this commandment was written. If husbands love their wives only with their natural love, the marriage is in trouble since natural love is centered on self and not on the wife. The home was intended to be a type of heaven on earth, not a type of hell on earth. The father is to be head, acting as the priest for his wife and children. He is to show them love and devotion. He is to pray for them. He is to lay hands on them when they are sick and claim the healing power of Jesus for them. He is to be a covering and protection for them. He is to give his life for them just as Jesus gave His life for the church. **Love wipes out** strife and envy. In a home where love abounds, you can eat a meal in peace and enjoy sweet fellowship.

Love in the Church

As the home life is, so will be the life of the local church and community. It is in the home that one learns to live the New Creation life. If he cannot live it in the home, he cannot live it any other place. He may fake it, but he cannot live it. This explains why the home is under such great satanic attack. If Satan can destroy the home, he can destroy the church.

Love Among Singles

I am thankful that a generation of young people is rising up who will not believe Satan's great lie that love is sex. They are believing God for a mate and waiting for the one God has chosen for them. They have become aware that the worldly system of dating is a rip-off and not of God. They are relating as brothers and sisters and not as potential mates. In this way they are not stealing affection which is not theirs. They are not getting hurt from broken hearts. They are not placing themselves in the position of yielding to the lusts of the flesh. They are being an example of purity.

How to Express Love

People are drawn to love. In these last days, God is bringing forth a people who will show His love to the world. They are not doing it through words, but in deed and truth, according to the Word of God.

"In this is love, not that we love God, but that He loved us and sent His Son to be the propitiation for our sins. Beloved, if God so loved us, we also ought to love one another." (I John 4:10–11, NAS)

This is love abundantly! Love is bearing one another's burdens, the strong holding up the weak (Romans 15:1). Love is taking time to fellowship with the fatherless young boy or girl (James 1:27). Love is repairing the car, washer, dryer, or whatever needs repairing for the brother or sister who cannot do that type of work.

Love is encouraging your brothers or sisters by being sensitive to their needs. Love is opening your home and your life to your brothers or sisters. Love is having all things in common. If I have something you need, you may use it and/or have it.

Love is realizing we are a product of God's love. We no longer have to fear failure because we can now love with His love. God's love never fails; therefore, we cannot fail.

The Warfare Against Love

However, we have self to contend with, and an enemy who wages war to keep God's love from coming forth. The following chart illustrates the enemy's means of keeping us from releasing God's love. The means by which we can overcome these weapons and allow God's love to prevail will be explored and demonstrated. The result: successfully waging spiritual warfare with the weapons of love. The victory: unselfishness.

Questions to Stimulate Thought and Revelation from the Lord

12. What is the supreme test to determine if one is truly a Christian? _____
13. How do we obtain true love? _____
    _____
14. Contrast Divine love and Human love. _____
    _____
    _____
15. How does faith operate? _____
16. Why can a Christian not fail? _____

16

Answers to Questions

1. He does not know God.

2. Because we love the brethren.

3. Laying down your life for a friend.

4. By Jesus laying down His life for us.

5. Lay our lives down for the brethren.

6. a. Suffers long
   b. Is kind
   c. Not jealous
   d. Does not brag
   e. Is not arrogant
   f. Does not act unbecomingly
   g. Does not seek its own
   h. Is not provoked
   i. Does not take into account a wrong suffered
   j. Does not rejoice in unrighteousness
   k. Rejoices with the truth
   l. Bears all things
   m. Believes all things
   n. Hopes all things
   o. Endures all things
   p. Never fails

7. The love of God.

8. Through the Holy Spirit.

9. a. Flesh and blood
   b. Against the rulers, powers, world forces of darkness, spiritual forces of wickedness in the heavenly places.

10. No.

11. Get water baptized, stop presenting self to sin, and instead present yourself as an instrument of righteousness and as a slave to righteousness.
    a. Reckon yourself dead unto sin but alive unto God through Jesus Christ
    b. Let not sin reign in your body
    c. Yield not your members as instruments of unrighteousness unto sin, but yield yourselves unto God
    d. Obey from the heart
    e. Yield your members servants to righteousness unto holiness

12. Whether or not we have love for others—living the Love Life.

13. Through the Holy Spirit—producing a relationship with God.

14. a. Gives—takes
    b. Other focused—self focused
    c. Never fails—always failing.

15. By love.

16. Because love never fails.

WEAPON

LOVE

TRAINING

**FAITH
&
TRUST**

WARFARE

ENVY
JEALOUSY
BITTERNESS
HATRED
UNFORGIVENESS

FEAR
MAN
AUTHORITY
PHOBIAS

COVETOUSNESS
DISCONTENTMENT
GREED
SELFISHNESS

VICTORY

SELFLESSNESS

CHAPTER THREE: ENVY

Jealousy Bitterness Hatred Unforgiveness

Envy Defined

On the preceding chart, we see one of the weapons Satan uses against love is envy. To be envious is to be jealous, resentful or uneasy with another's good fortune—to look upon his good fortune with enmity, malice, and bitterness.

Why People are Subject to Envy

People who have been recruited with a "come to Jesus and solve all your problems" religion are very vulnerable to this attack. It isn't too long before they become aware of the fact that they are still in the world with trials and tribulations. As they look around, it may appear that the wicked prosper better than they do. Some may even begin to long for the old way of living.

1. Why had the Psalmist almost stumbled and slipped?
   Ps. 73:2–3 a. _____
               b. _____

It is easy to forget very quickly how terrible the old way of living was as we are led into our wilderness experience. The enemy will launch his attack on us to bring us back into captivity. One of his most subtle and effective methods is to make us envious of sinners by creating a desire for old companionships. He covers up the hurts and bad experiences and magnifies the times of laughter and carefree moments. He seduces us into fantasies of the "good old days" when there was "plenty" to eat and drink.

2. How did the Psalmist win over envy of sinners?
   Ps. 73:17 _____

It must be settled in your heart once and for all: **God's way is the best and highest way regardless of the circumstances.** We are assured that if we seek first His kingdom and His righteousness, He will take care of our meat, drink, clothing, housing, money, and *all* other needs we have.

The Israelites forgot this during their journey in the wilderness when their food and water ran out. They began to speak to Moses about being brought into the wilderness to die. Then they began to long for Egypt where there were good things to eat. While it was true there were good things to eat in Egypt, it was deception for the Israelites to speak of eating them because all they had time for was making bricks. Their ration of food was meager and living conditions were intolerable. This was why they had cried out to God for deliverance in the first place.

The wilderness experience of Israel is a lesson for every Christian. God told the Israelites in Deuteronomy, chapter eight, that He had allowed this experience *to prove their heart*. In the same manner, He allows every Christian to come into circumstances *to prove their heart*, whether they will trust Him, obey Him and serve Him *for who He is* and not just for what He can give them.

The Result of Envy

We are not limited to only being envious of sinners. We can also be envious of other Christians and their blessings. One subtle method of the enemy in this regard is to expose certain weaknesses and failures in another person's life and then magnify these in comparison to their gifts from God. For example, a brother is inconsistent in controlling his temper, flying off the handle over trivial matters, and yet is used mightily of God to pray for the sick.

"How can this be," asks the enemy? "How can *he* be used like that? And when *you*, whose temper is controlled, pray for a sick person, instead of recovering that person becomes worse or may even die?"

Then there is sister-so-and-so who is a real busybody and spends a lot of time gossiping. In the meetings she has the most beautiful prophecies. "How can this be," asks the enemy? "How can *she* be used to prophecy like that? And when *you*, who do not gossip, try to prophecy or ask God for a word, the silence becomes unbearable." Beware! This type of thinking if not checked will lead to jealousness and bitterness which will spread like wildfire and defile your whole body and mind.

If one is not able to trust God and be patient with Him, but instead begins to agree with the envious spirit, he soon comes under bondage and enslavement to these desires with dire consequences.

3. What is the consequence of envy?
   Pr. 14:30 _____

An Example of Jealousy

A good example of jealousy is the story of Joseph in the book of Genesis. He had ten older brothers who tended the flocks. But his father gave him a coat of many colors that symbolized that he was the favorite son. His brothers became envious of his good fortune. Then God gave him a dream of his brothers bowing down to him. Joseph very unwisely told them of his dream and their envy turned into jealousy. A little later he had another dream and in this dream not only did his brothers bow down to him but his mother and father also bowed down to him. Again he related the dream. Now bitterness and hatred came upon his brothers and they plotted to kill him.

In the end, the dream was fulfilled when Joseph, as the Prime Minister of Egypt, received his brothers and family when they came seeking grain because of the famine in their country.

4. What does jealousy do to a man?
   Pr. 6:34 _____
5. What is the nature of jealousy?
   Song of Sol. 8:6 _____

20

Sheol is described in the scriptures as a land of darkness which consumes all beauty. It is a place of silence where praise and thanks are unknown. No wonder the enemy would attempt to put the saints of God under this bondage. In so doing, he stifles their beauty.

How Joseph Won Over Jealousy

In the story of Joseph we learn that his oldest brother kept the others from killing him. Instead, they sold him as a slave to a merchant trader who passed by where they were tending the flocks. The trader sold him to an army captain whose wife became attracted to Joseph and tried to seduce him. When he refused to be seduced by her, she falsely accused him of trying to rape her. Joseph was then unjustly put into prison. While in prison, he interpreted the dream of two inmates who had worked for Pharoah. He asked the one who was going to be freed to put in a good word for him with Pharoah. The inmate promised that he would, but failed to do so until several years later when Pharoah had a dream and could not obtain an interpretation from his advisors. The former inmate then remembered Joseph, told Pharoah, who had Joseph interpret his dream. Joseph interpreted Pharoah's dream of seven fat years followed by seven lean years of famine. As a result, he became second in command to Pharoah, who made him responsible for implementing a program to store up grain for the famine which was to come upon the land.

Then one day, his brothers who had wanted to kill him and who had sold him into slavery, came before him to ask for grain. They did not recognize Joseph but he knew they were his brothers. His response to them is one of the most beautiful acts of love and forgiveness in the Bible.

When Joseph revealed himself to his brothers the scriptures tell us that they were troubled, not knowing what to expect.

Joseph forgave his brothers and declared that it was not them who caused him to be in Egypt, but God. He did not say one word about being a slave or being in prison as a result of their deeds. In fact, he showed concern for them, being afraid they would be grieved and angry with themselves over their actions.

6. What are Christians commanded to do with regard to being wronged by others?
   Mk. 11:25 _____

We as Christians are commanded to have this type of attitude toward those who wrong us. I used Joseph as an example to do away with the suggestion that Jesus could forgive because of who He was but we can't because we are only human. God does not command us to do the impossible when He states that we must forgive others if we want our trespasses or sins forgiven.

Why We Must Forgive Others

It is of great interest to note that Jesus only explained one part of the prayer that is commonly referred to as "The Lord's Prayer." In Matthew 6:14–15 (NAS) we read, "For if you forgive men for their transgressions, your Heavenly Father will also forgive you: but if you do not forgive men, then your Father will not forgive your transgressions."

It is very easy to be resentful and unforgiving of others, especially loved ones. You are, of course, going to forgive them. But first they need to be taught a lesson—so you pout for a few days. In so doing, you are giving place to the devil.

21

7. What is the result of unforgiveness?
   Matt. 18:33–35 _____

In chapter 18 of Matthew, Jesus used the story of a servant who owed a huge debt. But the servant had no money with which to settle his account. His master had mercy on him and forgave him the debt. But then the servant went out and met someone who owed him a small debt. He asked for payment of the small debt, but when the debtor was unable to pay and asked him for patience, the servant responded by having the man who owed him this tiny debt cast into prison. When his master heard of this, he called the servant and told him that he should have had compassion and pity such as had been shown to him. The master was angered and delivered him to the tormentors. In Matthew 18:35 (NAS) He says, "So shall My Heavenly Father also do to you, if each of you does not forgive your brother from your heart."

How You Forgive Others

It is not easy to forgive someone from the heart who has just wronged us and treated us unfairly without a just cause for their actions. Every time we recall the incident(s), strong emotions and feelings rise up within us and we find ourselves wishing there was some way we could avenge ourselves. "How can I possibly forgive when I feel the way I do?" Forgiveness, praise the Lord, is not an emotion, but *an exercise of the will*. It is *a choice, not a feeling*. We choose to forgive, and in so doing, we say to our emotions and feelings, "You are not my Lord; Jesus is my Lord. I refuse to serve you anymore in this matter. I choose God's way. I fall out of agreement with unforgiveness. I choose to forgive and in the name of Jesus, I do forgive."

Each time our emotions and feelings try to take over, we need to resist them in the name of Jesus, recalling the choice we made to obey God rather than emotions and feelings. If they persist, we just ask Jesus to *heal our memories* and to *heal us inwardly* so that Satan cannot continue to torment us through our memories.

8. In what manner are we to forgive others?
   Col. 3:13 _____

There are two words in Colossians 3:13 which reach out and grip me: "*Just as* Christ forgave you, so also should you." The Lord revealed to me that when I first came to Him and became a believer, I wasn't asking Him to respond to me according to right and wrong; nor was I asking Him to deal with me according to just and unjust. No, I needed mercy. I needed forgiveness. If God had dealt with me in any way other than His grace and mercy, there would have been no forgiveness.

How could God forgive me for living for Satan rather than Him? How could God forgive me for being the cause of His Son's crucifixion? There was nothing right about it. There was nothing just about it.

Even as Christ forgave me, so also should I. Christ forgave me because He *chose to do so*. It had nothing to do with right or wrong, just or unjust. He loved me, and this love allowed Him to choose to forgive.

Why Satan Does Not Want You to Forgive

Satan is no dummy. In fact, he was once the angel of wisdom. He knows the scriptures and attempts to use them to his advantage. If he can create a situation wherein we are wronged, he will do so with the intent of then waging war to keep us from forgiving the trespass or sin as commanded by God. His purpose in keeping us from forgiving others is two-fold: 1) **it separates us from God and brings us under the bondage of sin;** 2) **unforgiveness gives him a legal right to inflict torment.** (See Matthew 18). This makes unforgiveness the doorway to untold torment. It seems that nearly everyone has been snared by this method of the enemy.

Various Forms of Unforgiveness

Unforgiveness comes in various forms, the most common being a personal wrong. In some cases it may be political (broken promises or passage of a certain law), ethnic (advantages afforded one group over another), religious (excluded by some group or witnessed to wrongly).

Many people have unforgiveness toward God. They have attributed certain acts to be from God. Seeing no justification for God to act in such a manner, or to permit such actions, they develop resentment toward God. This brings themselves under the bondage of unforgiveness.

Unforgiveness toward God is indeed a tragedy when we consider the love and forgiveness God has toward us. He demonstrated His love and forgiveness by becoming flesh and dying to set us free from the bondage of Satan.

9. Who is the author of sickness?
   Matt. 12:22 _____
   Matt. 17:15–18 _____
   Lk. 13:16 _____
10. Who is the author of death?
    Heb. 2:14 _____

A God who loved enough to die for us wants nothing less than the *very best* for our lives. He is not the author of sickness, but the healer. He is not the author of death, but the resurrection. If all the selfishness in the world was removed we would not have the tragedies of wars, killings, sicknesses, and injustices.

Another form of unforgiveness is toward self. Many times a person can accept God's forgiveness, but continues to be under bondage of the condemnation of self, not forgiving himself.

11. According to Rom. 8:1, where is there no condemnation?
    _____

How to Receive God's Forgiveness

Others find themselves unable to receive God's forgiveness because the enemy keeps bringing up past sins and ministering condemnation to them. These believers wrongly accept this as an indication that God has not really forgiven them. They do not understand *a very basic and a very freeing truth*, which can not be stressed enough: **our sin is always against God, not others, self or Satan.** Others may be wronged or hurt by our actions, but sin is against God. This makes sin none of Satan's business, even though he does try to stick his nose into it. And since our sin is not against others or self either, self has no say so in it. Only God has this right to say anything, so we need to listen to what He has to say, such as in I John 1:9.

12. If we confess our sin, what will God do?
    I John 1:9 _____

If we are cleansed from all unrighteousness, then we must be righteous. The word righteous means in right-standing with God. He puts us back into right standing with Him. Whether Satan or self likes it or not, doesn't make one bit of difference. They do not have a say in the matter. We need to listen only to what God has to say, such as in Psalm 103:12 and Isaiah 43:25.

13. How far does God remove our sins when He forgives us?
    Psalm 103:12 _____

14. What is God's attitude toward remembering our forgiven sins?
    Isaiah 43:25 _____

There is a reason for using east and west rather than north and south. The distance from north and south can be measured as there is a north pole and a south pole. There is no way to measure the distance from east to west, and that is how far our sin is removed.

In Isaiah we are told that God not only forgives, He remembers our sins no more. This is a very freeing truth because if after asking forgiveness, we find our sin being brought to our attention, we know the source must be the enemy because God has said that He Himself remembers them no more. Remember, the objective of Satan in bringing up a forgiven sin is to place us under condemnation and keep us out of fellowship with our Father—one of the snares of the enemy.

Four Steps to Victory

Practically speaking, there are four steps we can follow to achieve this victory. The first step toward victory is realizing we *can* forgive. It is a definite and specific *choice* we can make. It may not be an easy choice. In fact, it may be quite painful, but it is a decision we can make. Our emotions and feelings may not agree with the decision and they can even react violently in opposition to it. However, **emotions and feelings are not lord. Jesus is Lord** and He is the One to obey. Therefore, to forgive is to exercise our will in obedience to the Word of our Lord Jesus Christ.

The second step is to understand we *need* to forgive others when we are wronged. We are told to forgive. In some areas, we may not want to obey. If we don't, we are open to torment. Also, if we do have bitterness, resentment, or other negative feelings toward the person or persons, we must confess them and ask for forgiveness, ourself.

The third step is to *declare* the sin, the wrong, the trespass, and the person or persons we are forgiving. If more than one act is involved, we need to name each separate act and forgive each one.

Fourth, ask the Father to *heal us of memories and hurts* and fill us with love and compassion toward the person(s). This is critical because the enemy will wage war against our mind to bring us back under the bondage of sin. His method is to use subtle thoughts and suggestions to recreate the situation by which we were originally snared. It is vital that we refrain from bringing up our forgiveness to *ourself, anyone else,* or to *the person* we have forgiven.

Thoughts will arise to evoke strong emotional responses. But because our memories have been healed, our initial response will not be as before. However, if the thought is not "taken captive to Christ" but allowed to run free in our mind, it will begin to spread like cancer. Before too long it will have reopened the wounds which were healed and again bring us under the bondage of sin.

Because the attacks begin in a soft and gentle way, then grow if unchecked, it is important to catch the first offender and deal with it.

One way of doing this is to ask the Holy Spirit to sound the alarm in us the moment any such activity begins. When the Holy Spirit sounds the alarm we must then respond *immediately*!

It is on the same order of catching a thief attempting to burglarize a home or business. He trips the alarm and the police rush to the scene to arrest him before he gets away. If he isn't captured, he is free to come back again and again. It may be the next time he will get away with the robbery.

Therefore, the imagination or thought must be dealt with quickly or it will escape and come back again and again with the purpose of weakening our resistance. Once this happens, and we are weakened, the enemy will launch an all out attack to try to completely overwhelm and capture us.

If we have not totally and completely forgiven someone, the enemy has a legal right to attack in this manner. However, if we have been obedient, to forgive from the heart, then victory is assured. We counterattack with our weapon of love, releasing love to the one we have forgiven. The attacks will grow weaker and weaker until they are gone.

It should be mentioned here that it is not unusual to come face to face with the one whom we have forgiven and be tempted to stir up old memories and emotional responses. At this time, the need for compassion toward that person is the greatest. We need to ask God to allow us to look on them with the compassion of Jesus so that when they see our eyes and look into our face, they will *see and experience* the love and compassion of Jesus.

One last important point: our forgiveness may or may not result in a change of behavior in the other person. Also, it can happen in some cases that the ones we have forgiven may even get worse instead of better in their attitude toward us. This also can be used by the enemy. Even though we have been obedient and we have forgiven them, they continue as before. We must remember that God has not commanded forgiveness to be made in order to change the other person. Rather, *God has commanded forgiveness in order that we might be freed from the consequences of unforgiveness* and brought into the image of Jesus.

Questions to Stimulate Thought and Revelation from the Lord:

15. Why does God allow Christians to come into a "wilderness" experience?

_____

_____

16. How can you keep from being envious of sinners and other Christians?

_____

_____

17. How did Joseph handle the wrong done to him by his brothers?

_____

_____

18. List various forms of unforgiveness.

_____
_____
_____
_____

19. List four steps to take in forgiving.
    a. _____
    b. _____
    c. _____
    d. _____

20. Why should you not think upon and/or discuss your forgiveness?

_____
_____

21. If you have been snared with any of these subjects, pray this prayer or one similar to it:

    Father, I ask You to forgive me for allowing [name what it is—envy, resentment, unforgiveness] to be in my heart. I now make a decision of my will to no longer yield to this influence. I ask You, Lord Jesus, to strengthen me inwardly through the power of the Holy Spirit that by Your love and through Your love I am walk in victory. I thank you in Jesus Name, Amen.

Answers to Questions

1. a. He was envious of the arrogant.
    b. He saw the prosperity of the wicked.

2. He came into the sanctuary of God and perceived their end.

3. Rottenness to the bones.

4. Jealousy enrages a man.

5. Severe as Sheol.

6. Forgive them.

7. He will turn you over to the tormentors until the debt is paid.

8. Just as the Lord forgave us.

9. Satan.

10. The devil.

11. *In* Christ Jesus.

12. He will forgive us our sins and cleanse us from all unrighteousness.

13. As far as the east is from the west.

14. He will not remember them any more.

15. To prove our hearts: whether or not we will trust, obey and serve Him for who He is—not just for what He can give us.

16. Agree with God regardless of circumstances.

17. He forgave them and was concerned for them and how they might feel.

18. Towards God, towards self, towards others.

19. Realize we can forgive, understand we need to forgive, declare the sin and persons involved to the Lord, ask for healing of the memories and hearts.

20. They can reopen wounds and lead us back to unforgiveness and the bondage of sin.

CHAPTER FOUR: FEAR

Man   Authority   Phobias

Fear Defined

On the chart on page 17 we learn that another weapon Satan uses against love as a weapon is fear. Fear is a perverted spiritual force which operates through the law of sin (Rom. 7:23) and produces great torment. The first example we have of fear in operation in the Bible demonstrates how it destroys faith and separates us from God.

The Origin of Fear

In the beginning Adam walked with God, talked with God, and enjoyed sweet communion and fellowship with God in the garden of Eden. He completely *trusted* and had *faith* in God in every area of his life.

One day, Satan came to Adam's wife, Eve, and seduced her into disobeying God's command to not eat of the fruit of the tree of knowledge of good and evil. She then gave some of the fruit to Adam who was there with her and he also ate.

After this act of disobedience, God again came to the garden (Gen. 3:7–10) and called Adam. This time, instead of looking forward to talking with God, Adam tried to hide from God and had to admit to God that he was afraid. Sin had allowed fear to come into their heart and Adam could no longer trust God, but instead feared Him. God had not changed, but Adam was no longer the same.

We need to know what God says regarding fear:

1. Who is *not* the author of fear?
   II Tim. 1:7 _____
2. If God is not the author of fear, who is?
   II Tim. 1:7 _____
3. What is fear?
   II Tim. 1:7 _____
4. What does fear involve?
   I John 4:18 _____
5. What are you to do with fear?
   I John 4:18 _____

Fear is a means the enemy uses to keep the love of God from being manifested. In Timothy, fear is referred to as a spirit, and in John we are told fear is to be case out. This is the way we are to handle all spirits that are not of God—cast them out.

The scriptures teach that the blood of Jesus *cleanses* us from sin, the flesh is to be *crucified*, and evil spirits are to be *cast out* by the name of Jesus. This makes it clear that we can not crucify a spirit any more than we can cleanse one. They must be dealt with in the manner revealed in God's Word if victory is to be realized—i.e., cast them out.

The Results of Fear

6. Who shall have a part in the second death?
   Rev. 21:8 a. _____ b. _____
   c. _____ d. _____
   e. _____ f. _____
   g. _____ h. _____

The first person listed is one who is cowardly, which is the same as fearful. This scripture contrasts with verse 7 which speaks of *the overcomer* who will inherit the things of the kingdom of God, being a son of God. What is he overcoming? The things listed in verse 8, of which the first is fear. God hates fear so much that those who allow it to dominate their life head the list of those who will be cast into the lake that burns with fire and brimstones. But he that overcomes, including overcoming fear, shall inherit the kingdom of God.

Fear is a vicious torment in spirit that is spoken about in some form of "FEAR NOT" 366 times in the Bible. Since there are only 365 days in a year except for leap year, God has made provision for His People to serve Him every day without fear.

7. How are we to serve God?
   Lk. 1:74–75 _____

It is interesting to note that being delivered from the hand of our enemies allows us to serve God without fear and in holiness and righteousness all our days.

It should be further noted that fear is used not only to keep one from entering the kingdom of God but it is also used to keep believers who have entered from experiencing what is rightfully theirs as a result of being in the kingdom of God. Fear cripples Christians in many ways to prevent them from witnessing to others the manifold love of God. Consider healing, baptism in the Holy Spirit, prosperity, and other provisions which rightfully belong to all Christians, but which many do not possess because of fear.

8. What has the Father chosen gladly to give His flock?
   Lk. 12:32 _____

9. What is the condition for receiving the kingdom?
   Lk. 12:32 _____

10. What are two things God desires for all believers?
   3 Jn. 2 _____

11. What is the condition for prospering and good health?
   3 Jn. 2 _____

How Fear Affected Job

We learn even more about fear from the many examples in the scriptures of how God dealt with the people and their leaders in this area of fear. One book of the Bible that is devoted to fear and its consequence is the book of Job.

12. What had come upon Job?
    Job 3:25 _____

13. What instruments did Satan use to attack Job?
    Job. 1:15, 16, 17, 19; 2:7
    a. (1:15) _____ b. (1:16) _____
    c. (1:17) _____ d. (1:19) _____
    e. (2:7) _____

In Job 1:10 Satan declares there was a hedge around Job and his house and all that he had, on every side. Job was living in prosperity and so were his children. However, Job had a problem; He began seeing *fear images*. In his thinking he began to entertain thoughts of disaster and "what if's." He could see poverty, sickness, disease, and calamity coming upon him and his children. He was praying daily that these would not come, but it was not out of faith he was praying, but out of fear. The very things Job feared and was afraid of were the very things which came upon him. Fear broke down the hedge God had placed around Job and all that he had. But Job's story has a beautiful ending with everything being restored two fold. In fact, according to James 5:11, this outcome reveals that the Lord is full of compassion and is merciful.

How Fear Affected Abraham

Abraham could not see as God saw. He saw himself childless and without a heir. God saw him as a father of nations. To help Abraham overcome his wrong image of himself and to stand against the fear that God would not keep his promise he told him to look at the stars and visualize them as his descendants. Thus, God replaced fear images with faith images. Furthermore, He gave Abraham the image of Himself being a shield to him.

14. According to Gen. 15:1-2, how did Abram see himself? _____
    _____

15. What method did God use to get Abram to see himself differently? Gen. 15:5
    _____
    _____

16. How did God counteract Abram's fear? Gen. 15:1 _____
    _____

17. How did Abram respond? Gen. 15:6 _____
    _____

Abram turned his eyes away from the natural circumstances, which were giving him fear images, to the promises of God, which produced faith images—and faith perfected him in love. When he began seeing himself according to the Word of God, he could trust in God and His Word. When the enemy came with fear, doubt, and unbelief Abram would look up at the stars and smile because he knew something the enemy did not know. He knew God loved him and that he loved God. As Abram was perfected in love, the promises of God came to pass. When he and his wife were too old to have children, for Abram was one hundred years old, a son whom they named Isaac (laughter) was born to them.

How to Overcome Fear

From the example of Job and Abraham, it is evident that fear is a weapon used by the enemy to tear down God's protection and covering for those who are trusting Him.

As we read in I John 4:18, love casts out fear and **one who fears has not yet been perfected in his love relationship with God. In yielding to fear the door is open to torment and punishment. Consequently, the soul cannot prosper and the conditions for living in prosperity and health have been done away with.**

18. List what cannot separate us from the love of God. (Rom. 8:35, 37–39)

a. _____ b. _____

c. _____ d. _____

e. _____ f. _____

g. _____ h. _____

i. _____ j. _____

k. _____ l. _____

m. _____ n. _____

o. _____ p. _____

q. _____

God's love for us is unchangeable. He loves us as much today as He will tomorrow, and if God be for us, who can be against us? *His love guarantees us success.* We are a product of God's love and love never fails; therefore, we cannot fail.

One of the most beautiful scriptures defining God's love and care for us is Psalm 91. Read this Psalm and accept it as your insurance policy from God.

A further revelation of how all inclusive is God's love, care and protection comes from the account of how God led the Israelites out of Egypt to bring them into the land He had promised them. They had to exercise great trust in God's Word as spoken through His prophets. They had no jobs, houses, or land. There was no government to protect them or army to fight for them. All they had was the Word of God.

We also have the Word of God which is sealed by the blood of Jesus, making it a better covenant. Therefore, we can *boldly* enter into the promises which are ours in Christ Jesus.

Fear is not for God's people. It is only for His enemies. God has promised us that we are to possess this world and *rule and reign* with our Lord Jesus Christ. He has given us His Word that health, wealth, and life are ours because Jesus has made these provisions for us.

This world was not created for the devil and his kind. It was created by Jesus—for Him and His people. And His people, by training in faith and trust, release love that casts out all fear. We need to do away with fear and its torment. We need to let the love of Jesus reign in our hearts with full assurance that all the promises of God are yea and amen in Jesus.

19. Who will supply all your needs and how will He do it? (Phil. 4:19)

a. _____

b. _____

20. Who has carried away all your sickness and how did He heal you?

Is. 53:5 _____

I Pet. 2:24 _____

Two Methods Used to Produce Fear

There are two methods employed by the enemy to bring fear upon someone; the *ear gate* and the *eye gate*. Satan is constantly seeking a means into the believer's thought life—the battlefield is the mind—through what he hears and sees.

In this day and time, everyone is given ample opportunity to be snared by fear. Inflation, unemployment, crime, social injustices, moral decline, pollution, energy crises, and world unrest are just a few of the prevailing circumstances to bring fear upon people. Jesus declared in Luke 21:26 that the hearts of men would fail and their courage would yield to panic as a result of fear from seeing what was coming upon the earth.

21. How is the Christian not to walk, and how is he to walk? (II Cor. 5:7)

a. _____

b. _____

To not walk by sight means to not make decisions according to material and physical circumstances. To walk by faith is to make decisions based exclusively upon God's Word. Faith and God's Word are synonymous as we shall see in our study of the weapon of faith

22. What does God command every son to do? (Pr. 4:20–21)

a. _____

b. _____

23. What are the two results of obeying in verse 22?

_____ and _____

The command to keep God's Word in the midst of our heart is accomplished through giving attention (seeing) to His Word and inclining our ear (hearing) to what He is saying. In so doing we will live in health and prosperity, because faith comes by hearing and hearing by the Word of God. (Rom. 10:17).

Let us now look at an example of how fear is introduced through the ear gate and eye gate and how love (faith and trust in God's Word) responds.

24. What did Saul and his soldiers see and hear? (I Sam. 17:4–10)

a. _____ b. _____

25. What was the result? (I Sam. 17:11)

a. _____, b. _____

Goliath was over nine feet tall and his armor weighed more than most soldiers could carry, much less fight in. When he spoke his words of challenge into the *ears* of men *not prepared* in their hearts by the *love* of God, *fear* struck them. They were dismayed. Their knees smote together and their heart leaped up into their throat and seemed frozen in place. Their courage disappeared, leaving them limp as a wet noodle.

How David Handled Fear

Into the midst of this fear-filled army walked a young man named David who had some older brothers in the army. His father had sent him to find out how they were doing and to give them some goodies from home.

26. What was David's response to what he saw and heard? (I Sam. 17:23–26)
    a. _____
    b. _____
27. How did King Saul feel about David?
    I Sam. 17:33 _____
28. How did David handle the fear, doubt, and unbelief spoken to him by King Saul?
    I Sam. 17:34–37 _____
29. Why did David refuse to use King Saul's armor?
    I Sam. 17:38–39 _____
30. What tactic did the enemy use against David? (I Sam. 17:42–44)
    a. _____
    b. _____
    c. _____
31. How did David counter-attack?
    I Sam. 17:45–47 _____
32. What was the result?
    I Sam. 17:50–51 _____

David heard and saw what everyone else was experiencing, yet his response was totally different. Through his experience tending sheep he had *developed a personal love relationship with God* which nothing could quench. He was *so in love with God* that when he saw Goliath putting God to shame through snaring Saul and his army with fear, righteous indignation came over him. Faith arose in his heart and *David went on the offensive* instead of drawing back in fear. He was not moved by the seeing and hearing of the natural circumstances, because he walked not by sight but by faith. David responded to Goliath out of his love relationship with God.

We must also learn to respond to the Goliaths which come out to challenge our love relationship with Jesus. We are living in an age of fear. This has been vividly dramatized when gasoline shortages have occurred. Some people were reported to have waited for hours in line at gas stations to purchase less than one dollar's worth of gas.

A Modern Day Example of Handling Fear

I had an opportunity to war against fear one time during a truck strike. It was reported that our grocery stores were running out of milk and bread. My son came home from school with several stories of families buying up all the bread and milk they could purchase. He thought we should rush out and buy ours before it was too late. I looked in the refrigerator and we still had enough milk to last one more day, and the same was true for our bread. I talked to my son about God's promises. By faith we claimed the bread and milk we would need the next day.

As I returned home from work the next day, I stopped at the store and bought milk and bread. When I came home and showed my son what God had done, we had a beautiful "Thank-you Lord Jesus" session.

33. What two things have never been seen? (Ps. 37:25)
    a. _____
    b. _____

Another fear, the fear of authority, keeps the saints of God from health and prosperity. This type of fear keeps them from experiencing blessings which are rightfully theirs in both "secular" work and ministry in the kingdom of God. In some cases it is fear of authority that prevents them from excelling in their job responsibilities and enjoying the prosperity which comes as a result of salary increases and promotions.

34. Who is the source of all authority?
    Rom. 13:1 _____

35. If you resist authority, who are you resisting?
    Rom. 13:2 _____

36. What is the purpose of authority?
    Rom. 13:4 _____

37. How can you keep from fearing authority?
    Rom. 13:3 _____

These scriptures state that all authority and power is from God and, therefore, we do not need to fear those who are in a position of authority. If we are doing what is right, those in authority will have no reason to be offended or to punish us unjustly.

I can recall times when someone would tell me my boss wanted to talk with me and immediately fear would seize me. I would frantically search my memory to recall what I had done wrong. Who had I offended? What responsibility had I left undone? From there I would start thinking about where could I get another job and would anyone hire me if I was fired. After several minutes in the grip of fear, I would collect myself as best I could and slowly walk toward my boss's office. I hoped no one could see my shirt moving just over my heart, which was pounding so fast and loud it sounded like a jackhammer to me. I always tried to be cool, calm, and collected when I entered his office and saw him sitting behind his big desk which somehow appeared bigger than other times. I would desperately search his face to see if there was an indication of his mood. Was he angry? Upset? I always hoped my voice would not crack or quiver when I said in a matter of fact tone, "You wanted to see me, boss?"

Those times were bad enough. But I remember one time when my boss was in his boss's office and word came to me that they wanted to talk with me. I not only had the time in my own office to be assailed, but I also had to walk down the long hallway to the big boss's office. By the time I arrived I was about to have a heart attack. All they had in store for me was a letter of appreciation from the President of our company for a successful project I had accomplished, along with a check for several hundred dollars.

It was during these times that Jesus began dealing with me personally regarding my own *lack of trust in Him* which manifested itself through my fear of either losing my job or not doing a good job. As with Abram, He began turning my eyes and thoughts *to Him and His Word* rather than to my natural circumstances. Although I was excelling in my job to the point of receiving special recognition, fear blinded me from the truth of how God was blessing and prospering me. Because I was trusting in myself and my employer as my source, rather than God, the enemy was waging war against me and winning. However, as I began to move into the love realm and see God's love and faithfulness, my fear images turned into faith images. I began to see myself as a channel for God's talents and abilities to be expressed to others.

My professional training was in chemistry. One time I was supervising a production area which required chemical engineering abilities that I did not possess. But I personally knew the greatest engineer in the whole universe. He knows more than all the professors put together. Best of all, He loves me and wants me to succeed. And succeed I did because of some revelations He gave me in the spirit. The result was not only success—I also received four awards for engineering modifications that increased our production efficiency and cut costs.

This problem of fear of authority sometimes goes back to childhood days. Many times parents unwittingly open their children to fear of authority. For example, a parent may tell a child who is acting up that the policeman will get him rather than disciplining the child with love. If they are in a store, the parent may point to a man or woman and declare to the child, "that man over there will get you if you do not behave."

Teachers in school at times will use fear as a means of controlling their students. They use the threat of sending the unruly student to the principal or dean.

There are many examples of fear being used to produce a desired behavior in others. It is therefore not surprising to find many people with a fear of those in authority, expecting them to always be a threat to their peaceful life.

At the other extreme is a lack of respect for authority. This lack of respect will produce chaos, as we have seen in riots and also in parent-child and teacher-student conflicts, wherein the child has raised up in rebellion against authority.

Our Father tells us all authority exists because of Him. He delegates authority to maintain discipline and order. In the absence of authority there is confusion and every type of evil and disorder. Therefore, we recognize authority as being for our good.

How to Overcome the Fear of Sickness and Disease

Another area in which fear strikes is the fear of sickness and disease, especially if someone in the family has died as a result of a particular illness. For example, maybe your father died from cancer. Then every time an unusual pain occurs the suggestion comes, "I've got cancer; there is no cure; I'm going to die as my father died."
38. How can children avoid bearing their parents' iniquity?
    Ezek. 18:20 _____
39. How have we been delivered from the curse?
    Gal. 3:13 _____
If the enemy can get you to picture yourself having cancer and confessing that you will probably have cancer because your father did, then he can legally induce cancer into your body. (As previously shown with Job, what we fear will come upon us.) This is due to God's Word which says you have what you believe and confess (Mark 11:23).

If, on the other hand, you picture yourself living in health and confess your freedom from the curse, relying upon God's Word that you have been redeemed from the curse of the law by Jesus' death on the cross, you will effectively nullify this attack of the enemy.

How to Overcome the Fear of Phobias

I am constantly amazed at the various phobias people express—ranging from a fear of

34

of insects and heights, to crowds, animals, elevators, airplanes, cars, or just about anything you can name. The enemy has been successful in bringing this type of bondage upon a vast number of saints. In so doing, he has robbed them of many enjoyments and pleasures.

Again, for some, this type of fear was introduced when they were children. They were exposed through movies, television, and ghost stories. Others had some type of traumatic experience—a peaceful, loving family dog that the children played with that suddenly, and without warning, attacked them and they became terrified of dogs. For some, their fears have been inherited, passed down from one generation to the next and on to them. In all cases, the fear is genuine and something they had rather not have in their life.

The starting point is to begin drawing nigh to God and resisting the fear through Jesus' name. Then, go forward as much as you can. Each time you move forward, it is producing strength and reducing your fear.

For example, if you are afraid of heights, cast out the fear in Jesus' name. Next, begin seeing yourself climbing a ladder, standing on a wall, or looking down from a tall building. Then see yourself as not being afraid. Turn your fear images into faith images.

The Importance of Your Speech

Start now to declare with the psalmist, "The Lord is my light and my salvation; whom shall I fear? The Lord is the defense of my life; whom shall I dread?" (Psalm 27:1)

Begin to give attention to God's Word and keep it in the midst of your heart:

Matthew 10:30–31 "But the very hairs of your head are all numbered. Therefore do not fear, you are of more value than many sparrows."

Isaiah 43:1 ". . .Do not fear, for I have redeemed you; I have called you by name; you are Mine!"

Isaiah 41:10 "Do not fear, for I am with you; do not anxiously look about you, for I am your God. I will strengthen you, surely I will help you, surely I will uphold you with My righteous right hand."

These are just a sample of God's Word with regard to *fear not*. You can discover other verses. The ones which speak to you are the ones to hide in your heart, to dwell upon, and to keep you from being overcome by fear.

Practically speaking, we need to learn to speak out against the devil. We need to say, "Fear, I resist you in the name of Jesus. I refuse to fear. Doubt, I resist you in the name of Jesus. I refuse to doubt."

We can do it. If we can't, then God is a liar because He said that we could. We have the authority because Jesus gave it to us. He gave us His name!

Instead of our running, we will put the devil on the run. Instead of our being afraid of him, he will be afraid of us because we have discovered how to resist him by standing our ground on the truth of God's Word. We have learned who we are in Christ. We have found that I John 4:4 is true, "Ye are of God, little children, and have overcome them: because greater is He that is in you, than he that is in the world."

It is all in Jesus. You can be strong in Him, in His power, and in His might. It is not by anything we have done; it is by what He has done. God raised Him from the dead and gave Him a name that is above every name. That name now belongs to you and to me.

Start right now. Submit yourself to God. Immerse yourself in His love. Purge yourself of all sin. Resist the devil; stand your ground on the truth of God's Word regarding all fears and give no place to the devil. Resist him in the loving Lord Jesus' name.

Questions to Stimulate Thought and Revelation from the Lord

40. What was the effect of fear in Adam's relationship with God?

_____

41. Why does God hate fear? _____

_____

42. List some effects of fear. _____

_____

43. What two gates are used by Satan to introduce fear?
    a. _____ b. _____

44. What is God's method for dealing with fear?

_____

45. How can you stay free from fear? _____

_____

46. Now, list one or more scripture verses pertaining to your *"fear not"* that you shall put your trust in:

47. Write down your faith image; how you shall now see yourself:

48. If you are snared by fear, you need to be set free. Pray this prayer or one similar to it:

    In the name of Jesus, I take authority over the spirit of fear of _____
    (name of fear) and cast it out. In the place of fear, I release love into my soul. From this time
    forward I shall not be overcome by fear, but I shall draw nigh to my God in love and trust and
    resist fear in the name of Jesus.

Answers to Questions

1. God
2. The enemy (implied)
3. The opposite of power, love and sound judgment
4. Punishment
5. Love, so we can cast it out.
6. a. cowardly
   b. unbelieving
   c. abominable
   d. murderers
   e. immoral persons
   f. sorcerers
   g. idolators
   h. all liars
7. Without fear
8. The kingdom
9. Not being afraid
10. Prosperity and good health
11. The soul prospering
12. What he feared and dreaded
13. Sabeans attacked, Chaldean raids, Satan & boils, fire, great wind
14. Fearing God would give him nothing as he was childless and had no heir
15. Visualization of his descendants as the stars of the sky
16. Gave him a faith image of Himself being a shield to him
17. He believed
18. a. tribulation
    b. disaster
    c. persecution
    d. famine
    e. nakedness
    f. peril
    g. sword
    h. death
    i. life
    j. angels
    k. principalities
    l. things present
    m. things to come
    n. powers
    o. height
    p. depth
    q. any other created thing

19. God—in Christ Jesus
20. Jesus—by His scourgings and wounds
21. Not by sight; by faith
22. a. Incline our ears to His sayings
    b. Do not let them depart from our sight.
23. Life and health
24. a. A giant—Goliath
    b. Heard threats and a challenge
25. a. dismayed
    b. greatly afraid
26. a. What will be done for the man who kills this Philistine?
    b. Who is this uncircumsized Philistine that he should taunt the armies of God?
27. Only a youth
28. Recounted how the Lord had delivered him before
29. He was not personally tested in it
30. a. ridicule
    b. insult
    c. curse
31. Exalted God and said it was His battle
32. David killed Goliath
33. a. the righteous forsaken
    b. his descendants begging bread
34. God
35. God
36. To minister good to us from God
37. Do what is good
38. Don't walk as they did
39. By Jesus' hanging on the cross and becoming a curse for us
40. Caused him to hide
41. It prevents us from walking in faith, destroys faith, and separates us from God
42. Inhibit, prevent
43. a. ear
    b. eye
44. Turn fear images into faith images
45. Keep our eye on His Word and our ear inclined to His sayings

CHAPTER FIVE: COVETOUSNESS

Discontentment   Greed   Selfishness

Covetousness Defined

Another weapon used to prevent us from loving others as we should is covetousness. To covet means to desire and long for something belonging to another person. It is also a form of idolatry; it's love for money is described as the root of all evil and, according to Ecclesiastes 5:10, is never satisfied.

The Results of Covetousness

If left unchecked, covetousness can produce discontentment, greed and selfishness. Also, according to various scriptures, it can produce theft, lying, murder and apostasy; if not overcome, it can keep you out of heaven.

1. What is covetousness called? (Col. 3:5) _____

2. From the following scriptures list the action and result of covetousness.

	Action	Result
a. Joshua 7:11–26	_____	_____
b. II Kings 5:20–27	_____	_____
c. Acts 5:1–10	_____	_____
d. Ephesians 5:5	_____	_____

Various Forms of Discontentment

Discontentment may attack through negative feelings toward yourself, your spouse, children, parents, employer, employees and others. It may spring forth from your job, the place where you live, your lack of money, or anything that can induce you to be negative, critical and complaining.

Everyone has the ability to find something wrong with anything, at anytime, and in any place. Happy people simply refuse to do so.

The Main Source of Discontentment

One of the main roots to discontentment is looking within and seeing your own personal lack of talents, gifts and abilities. As you do, the suggeston is made that God really doesn't love and care for you as He does others.

This can cause you to think, "Perhaps God made a mistake in creating me;" "I'm not pretty;" "I do not talk right, walk right, laugh right, sing right, pray right;" "In fact, now that I think about it, there just isn't anything right about me." "I am too quiet," or "I am too loud;" "I am not very smart;" "Actually, now that I think about it, I am really dumb." "I can't learn very fast;" "I have a terrible memory;" "I don't relate well with others;" "I can't meet strangers." "Oh! if only I could be like so and so . . . they have so much going for them. The Lord has really blessed them."

Beware! This is spiritual warfare. It is a subtle attack of covetousness and discontentment. If not overcome it will lead into self-hatred, which is in reality a hatred of God and bitterness toward Him.

The Unique You

One of the ways to be an overcomer is to realize a very simple truth: You are a unique creation of God; there is not another person like you; someone may look like you, but no one else is endowed with your special attributes. For example, no one else has your fingerprints—they are uniquely yours!

If God had desired for you to look, walk, or talk differently, He would have created you differently. The truth is that God knew exactly what He was doing and the kind of person He wanted when He created you.

How to Overcome a Poor Self Image

Another truth to think upon is how much God loves, accepts and thinks about you. The scriptures reveal that God thinks highly of people; He made them in His image. Ephesians 2:10 declares we are His workmanship. The idea conveyed in the original language is that of a poem. We are a poem composed by God.

Every person has strengths and weaknesses. The good news is that the weakness of God is stronger than even the strength of man.

To avoid the trap of comparing yourself to others begin to realize that through Christ Jesus each of us have been given the ability to please God in a way that no one else can.

Therefore, seek ways that you can uniquely please God; as you begin to see yourself as the unique creation of God, to bring Him glory, praise, honor and pleasure, victory begins.

Continue in victory by seeing how you are one with Jesus. Meditate upon what this union means—all His wisdom, ability, and talents are available to you. Realize that He desires for you to prosper and be successful.

This will result in a desire to please Him rather than self. You will seek after His interest and not your own.

In so doing, you are walking in the love realm . . . you are exercising faith and trust in Jesus. Remember, love never fails.

3. Who created you? (Ps. 139:14) _____

4. Why were you created? (Rev. 4:11 KJ) _____

5. What are you in Christ? (II Cor. 5:17) _____

6. Who orders your steps? (Ps. 37:23–24) _____

7. Who will perfect that which concerns you? (Ps. 138:8) _____

39

8. Who has begun a good work in you and who will complete it? (Phil. 1:6) _____
9. By what means are you what you are? (I Cor. 15:10) _____

From these scriptures God reveals that you were created by Him and for His pleasure. He watches over you, orders your steps, perfects you, has made you a new creation in Christ Jesus.

Begin to confess what God says about you and not what the devil suggests. There is the power of life and death in the tongue. Let it be used to produce life and watch discontentment flee.

No matter what you were in sin and the kingdom of darkness, it has all passed away. Whatever your situation or circumstance is today can be changed for the better because all things have become new.

Various Forms of Greed

Although one normally thinks of greed as involving the desire for money, it is by no means limited to the dollar.

One may to be greedy for food, clothes, cars, houses, or other gains that are valuable to them.

It may also take the form of being eager to obtain promotions and recognition.

Regardless of the form it takes, greed must be recognized and overcome.

The Results of Greed

One of the most vivid examples of greed is the story of Judas. The scriptures tell us that Judas had a problem of covetousness. He became greedy for money and this led him into a disastrous decision.

10. From the following scriptures define what greed caused Judas to do:

John 12:5–6

a. _____

b. _____

Matt. 26:14–16

c. _____

Mark 14:10–11

d. _____

Matt. 27:3–5

e. _____

These scriptures give a vivid demonstration of spiritual warfare as stated in John 10:10: "The thief comes not except to steal, destroy and kill, but I am come that you might have life and that you might have it more abundantly."

How to Overcome Greed

Your life does not consist of the abundance of things which you possess. On the contrary, your life consists of the things which possess you. If you are possessed with obtaining material things, this becomes your lifestyle. If you are possessed with making money, this will become your life. On the other hand, if you are possessed with knowing Jesus and pleasing Him, then Jesus becomes your life.

This is not to imply one is to be passive and not advance in prosperity; it is not spiritual to be poor. In fact, it is not even scriptural.

11. What is poverty a result of? (Deut. 28:15–19) _____

12. What is poverty called? (Deut. 28:16–19) _____

13. What did Jesus do about the curse? (Gal. 3:13) _____

14. In what does God delight? (Ps. 35:27) _____

15. Whom does God prosper?
    a. (Ps. 122:6) _____
    b. (Ps. 1:1–3) _____

God has not declared money to be the root of all evil, but the love of money. He does not want us living in poverty and provided a way for us to be free from the curse of poverty. He delights in our prosperity; however, He also tells us to seek first His kingdom and righteousness and that He will take care of what we eat, drink, and wear.

Therefore, as we love God and fix our attention upon Him, trusting in Him, desiring nothing but Him, we will prosper and be successful without being greedy.

Selfishness Defined

Selfishness is the exclusive regard of a person for his own interests or happiness. It is supreme self-love or self-preference, which leads to action for the advancement of his own interest, power or happiness, without regarding the interests of others.

It is an interesting observation that the more one's heart is completely Jesus', the more liberal they become with their money and other possessions.

Selfishness stands in direct opposition to love, which is the giving of self without any conditions. As God is love, so man in his natural state is selfishness. Therefore, as he takes upon himself the nature of God he becomes benevolent.

Results of Selfishness

The results of Adam's transgression in the garden of Eden was the change of man's nature from that of benevolence to self-exaltation. When God called for Adam and confronted his sin, he immediately blamed his wife rather than acknowledging his wrong doing.

His son Cain followed in his footsteps and then one step further in killing his brother, Abel, who had brought the acceptable sacrifice to God.

A vivid portrayal of selfishness and how it operates is recorded in the book of Esther. Here is the story of a man named Haman who was so selfish and conceited that not only did he promote himself in the government but when Mordecai, a Jew, would not bow down as he passed by, he plotted and devised a scheme to kill all the Jews. In the end, his deeds caught up to him and he was hanged on the gallows he had prepared to hang Mordecai.

16. What is revealed about selfishness in Pr. 11:26? _____

17. What does God say about selfishness in Isa. 5:8? _____

18. What does Jesus say will be the result of selfishness in Matt. 25:41–46? _____

41

19. List the various forms of lovers mentioned in II Tim. 3:1–5:
    a. _____
    b. _____
    c. _____

In verse four it declares that these, plus the other attitudes listed, are a result of being lovers of self rather than lovers of God. In Philippians we are told that this selfishness seeks after self-interest rather than the interest of Jesus Christ.

How to Overcome Selfishness

According to I Corinthians 10:24 the way to avoid this snare is to begin seeking the good of others. This can only be accomplished by putting Christ first in our life and allowing His love to be manifested through us to others. In so doing, we will avoid the consequence of sin, poverty, and loss of spirituality which selfishness bring upon those who live under its bondage.

One way to begin the march toward victory in this warfare is to stop robbing God by not giving Him tithes and offerings.

20. What happens if you give tithes and offerings? (Malachi 3:10–11)
    a. _____
    b. _____
21. What happens if you rob God? (Malachi 3:8–9) _____

The Results of Giving

When I first became a Christian, I had a job earning $75 a week. My wife, baby and I were just barely getting along from payday to payday. We really did not have any money to put in the collection plate, so I would sort of tip God twenty-five or fifty cents. On rare occasions I might give Him a whole dollar. One day, I read a tract on the subject of tithing. In this tract the author spoke about believing in impossibilities. For example, the virgin birth is a biological impossibility and the resurrection is a physical impossibility. He stated that although Christians readily acknowledge belief in these two impossibilities they have difficulty with a mathematical impossibility—giving one-tenth to the Lord and living better on the nine-tenths than you could on the whole. For some reason this not only challenged me, it also made sense. If I could believe the first two, I could certainly believe the third as well.

We began tithing and somehow God did just what He had promised. For the first time we had money left over on our next payday. I thought, "this is really working, I'm going to try it again." So the next Sunday we put in our tithe and to my amazement we had money left over on our next payday. By this time I was becoming convinced that it pays not to rob God.

Then I discovered you could go beyond tithing into giving offerings and prosper even more. Down through the years we have given our tithes and offerings and God has opened the windows of heaven and met our every need.

Another blessing from this obedience is the promise to rebuke the devourer. Anytime I find little things beginning to go wrong with the car, stove, refrigerator or any other unexpected bills I immediately call out and ask God to rebuke the devourer as He promised. In this manner we are able to continually enjoy the blessings and not come under the curse.

22. To whom does all the silver and gold belong? (Haggai 2:8) _____
23. Who supplies you with money? (II Cor. 9:10) _____
24. If you sow sparingly, how shall you reap? (II Cor. 9:6) _____
25. If you sow bountifully, how shall you reap? (II Cor. 9:6) _____
26. What kind of giver does God love? (II Cor. 9:7) _____
27. What can affect your giving? (II Cor. 9:5) _____
28. What is the result of liberal giving? (II Cor. 9:11–14) _____
29. What is the result of all giving? (Luke 6:38) _____

From these scriptures it is no wonder that the enemy desires to keep a Christian from giving of himself and his money or other possessions. These passages tell us it not only keeps the gospel of the kingdom from being preached, it snares the believer and prevents him from obtaining the true riches in life.

The scriptures do not qualify giving; they do not place any limits or boundaries. In whatever manner you give it will be returned to you. This includes love, time, talents, abilities, friendship, giving a helping hand to someone in need, or any other way you may give to others.

Knowing this truth, it is not surprising to find the enemy waging war to snare the saints of God with selfishness. It is a means of robbing them from the blessings of God that are rightfully theirs. But, by training in faith and trust, learning how to live and walk in the love realm, victory over selfishness can be achieved.

Questions to Stimulate Thought and Revelation from the Lord

30. What is covetousness? _____
31. What is the most common means of discontentment? _____
_____
32. What are some ways in which God has made you a unique person? _____
_____
33. What are some unique ways you can please God? _____
_____
34. Name some forms of Greed _____
_____
35. Contrast love and selfishness _____
_____
36. Why does the enemy want people to be greedy and selfish? _____
_____
37. How can you get victory over these weapons of the enemy? _____
_____
38. If you have been snared in the area of covetousness, pray this prayer or one similar to it:

Father, I ask you to forgive me for not walking in the love realm and placing my faith and trust in you. And, in the name of Jesus and through the blood of Jesus, I break the power, dominion and influence of _____ (covetousness, discontentment, etc.) in my life and release the fruit of love. I ask the Holy Spirit to empower me to see myself as a unique creation of yours, made to give you pleasure, and show me ways to give of myself. In Jesus name, I pray—Amen.

Answers to Questions

1. Idolatry
2. Action
   a. Steal and deceive
   b. Lying
   c. Lying
   d. Idolatry
2. Results
   a. Make helpless before enemies
   b. Being cursed with leprosy
   c. Falling down dead
   d. No inheritance in the Kingdom of God
3. God
4. For God's pleasure
5. A new creation
6. God
7. God
8. God
9. By the grace of God
10. a. hypocrisy
    b. dishonesty
    c. treachery
    d. betrayed
    e. suicide
11. Disobeying God
12. A curse
13. Redeemed us from it
14. The prosperity of His saints
15. a. those who love Him
    b. those who delight in His law
16. Hoarding of food brings a curse
17. Woe to him
18. Go away into everlasting punishment
19. a. of self
    b. of money
    c. of pleasure
20. a. open windows of heaven and pour out blessings that there shall not be room enough to receive it.
    b. rebuke the devourer
21. Cursed with a curse
22. The Lord of Hosts
23. God
24. Sparingly
25. Bountifully
26. Cheerful
27. Covetousness
28. God is glorified and you are enriched in everything
29. In the same measure you give, it will be given unto you.
30. The desire and longing for something or someone belonging to someone else.
31. A poor self image
32. Your own personal answer applies
33. Your own personal answer applies
34. Money, food, clothes, material things, power, prestige
35. Love is the unconditional giving of self, while selfishness is the exclusive regard of a person for his own interest or happiness without regarding the interests of others
36. To rob them of the blessings of God that comes from giving
37. By training in faith and trust and learning how to live and walk in the love realm.

CHAPTER SIX: JOY

Joy Defined

A word used more often than it is understood is the word joy. To use joy successfully as a weapon to win in spiritual warfare requires clearing up some wrong understandings of just what it does mean.

Joy is not happiness. It is not an emotion or feeling. Rather, joy is a powerful spiritual *force* developed through praise and worship of God.

Happiness depends upon circumstances. Joy does not. If circumstances are good or bad, happiness will come or go because it is an emotion or feeling. Joy, however, is not limited by good or bad circumstances because it is free from emotions and feelings.

The Purpose of Joy

God did not design the Christian life to be lived under the domination of the soul, where emotions and the mind rule. He has given joy as a spiritual force to combat attitudes and remove roadblocks which keep one from living the abundant life Jesus gives. But joy is released only as one learns how to properly worship God—which is not an automatic accomplishment.

We should note that those who are controlled by their emotions and feelings—whether Christian or not—can only sing or laugh when things are going good, when everything is alright. One way to illustrate this is by contrasting the response of people at a ball game or concert to those in many churches. At the ball game they get caught up in the spirit of competition. They yell, clap their hands, stomp their feet and sing the team's fight song. A strong fan will drive hundreds of miles through the roughest of weather and lose hours of sleep and take time off from work to see his team play. If it is a good close game and goes into overtime, the fan will get so excited he can hardly stand it. If his team wins, it produces pure ecstasy.

This is not joy. It is a response of the soul and not the spirit.

Learning to emote to God may not be the easiest thing for some Christians. The first attempt at raising of the hands may result in only turning the palms upward. However, as one continues, soon they will be chest high, then shoulder high, and then on to the victory of being able to raise them high above the head unto God (Lam. 3:41).

The same may be true for clapping of hands. At first it may seem strange, but as one begins to submit the members of his body as members of righteousness to be used for the glory and praise of his Creator, it gets easier and easier (Psalm 47:1).

As people learn to emote to Jesus it isn't long until they discover ball games and other worldly events are not really all that exciting. In fact, they find it hard to emote toward those events because it far more exciting to emote to the Lord and soar up into the Heavens. Ball games, they discover, have no eternal significance.

How Joy is Released

Consequently, as one learns how to use his weapon of joy he discovers a release from the up and down roller coaster experiences produced by emotions and feelings. The Spirit of the Lord has set us free from the bondage of being controlled by an emotional response to our circumstances.

1. What is in the presence of God and at His right hand?
   Psalm 16:11 _____

Because Jesus lives right inside us, in our spirit, we are in His presence twenty-four hours a day. Therefore, we have fullness of joy in our spirit. We do not have to seek for joy, work for joy, sing for joy, leap for joy or any such thing, because we already have joy in full measure. However, to experience this joy we must **learn to release it from the bondage of our emotions and feelings.** Christians who have learned to so release joy are the happiest people on earth. What they have "learned" is how to praise and worship God and not things of God, or things of the world. When praises to God are going forth it releases one into the presence of God—thus releasing the spiritual force joy to counter attack the mind and emotions.

Releasing Joy in the Church

But what about the church? Well, usually there is not that much to get excited over. Even when someone gets saved, or healed or filled with the Spirit or shares a blessing, many "feel" it is improper to get excited or caught up in the Spirit of the Lord. After all, one must be sober before the Lord. I am not sure how this happened because when you read about heaven in the book of Revelation it appears to be a pretty noisy place. Angels singing and shouting, elders falling down and praising God, lots of shouting with loud voices. (Revelation 4:9–11).

Somewhere, someplace, somehow, the enemy has robbed the church of being able to get "caught up" in the Spirit and therefore not able to enter into true praise and worship. In many churches it is not acceptable to use your emotions and feelings in expressing praise, love, and adoration to the King of Kings and Lord of Lords, to the Creator of this universe. But as we shall see, proper praise and worship are essential to experiencing true joy.

2. For what purpose were all things created? (Revelation 4:11 (KJV))

   _____

Other translations use "because of Thy will" instead of pleasure. In either case, it was God's will or pleasure to create emotions and feelings for Himself, not for the pleasure of self or the world.

In a church service where the people have been freed by the Spirit it is not unusual to have a service begin with an hour or more of praise and worship. Out of this comes forth mighty manifestations of the presence of God because God inhabits the praise of His people (Psalm 22:3).

My first exposure to true emoting to God at a church service came some years ago when a small country church asked me to conduct a weekend revival. I had done some lay speaking on several occasions but not a revival. Consequently I was worried about finding something to speak about for five straight meetings. Furthermore, I knew they wanted to hear preaching instead of straight teaching and I did not consider myself a preacher. However, I believed God was in the invitation and figured it had something to do with my recent experience of being baptized in the Holy Spirit.

I was apprehensive as I drove down a winding, hilly road past houses and fields into a valley where the church sat back at the foot of a large hill. It was a small block building and did not really look too much like a church. I noticed on top of the hill someone had placed three crosses made out of tree limbs.

I parked my car, took a deep breath, got out and started walking toward the church. Because I was early it surprised me to see so many cars already parked around the church. I thought they must be having a committee meeting. At my church, almost everyone came at the last minute or even a little late unless they were on a committee and had to meet before the church service.

Nervous and wondering how I was going to make it through the first meeting, I opened the door and entered the building. It was almost filled with people. They all seemed so happy. I could hear people talking and laughing; a young mother was hugging her baby; a small boy was squirming in his seat. The platform was set up with a place for the choir on one side and on the other side I noticed a set of drums. The drums disturbed me and I wondered if someone was going to play them. Surely not, I thought. They were probably left there from a teenagers' meeting. I was immediately greeted warmly by some men, one of whom hurried off for the pastor to let him know I had arrived.

The pastor was in his late sixties, a short, round, bouncing bundle of joy. He bounced out from somewhere in back of the platform with a smile that said welcome. He began assuring me we were going to have a great meeting and that everyone was excited over my being with them. I hoped they would feel the same way when the meeting was over.

He took me over and introduced me to a family who was going to provide the special music. The father was a slender, curly headed man. On his face was an expression of joy and contentment. His wife had long red hair and a ready smile. They had two teenage boys who looked fairly typical. One was tall and lanky and you could tell he was growing so fast he was having some problems keeping his coordination. The younger one was all boy living in his own world. They all seemed to be full of the love of Jesus.

I didn't know it at the time, but later we were to be together in a week-long revival in Jackson, Michigan where we would discover how much we loved each other in Christ.

I soon made the amazing discovery that the drums were not left over from another meeting, but they were actually going to be played by the younger son. The elder son played a bass guitar while the father played lead guitar and the mother played the piano.

They led the congregation in singing. People began to clap their hands in time with the music. At first, the noise was bothersome. I had never been in a church where they used more than an organ and piano for music. And no one would dare clap their hands.

I was beginning to adjust to the noise when they did something else which was strange and upsetting. At the end of one of the songs, people began to raise their hands over their heads and worship and praise Jesus out loud. I looked at the man next to me. He had his eyes closed, arms extended upward and there seemed to be a glow on his face. He was talking to Jesus as if He was right there. The man's expression of love and adoration was slightly embarrassing to me.

At first, I was so caught up in the newness of everything that I was unaware of the time. However, when we sat down to listen to the family sing their songs, I glanced at my watch. I could hardly believe my eyes. We had been singing for over forty-five minutes. That, plus the special music, would take up all the time and I would not have any time to preach.

I began to panic just a little trying to figure out how to speak in five or ten minutes. Then as the special music began to go on and on, I really started to panic. Time was passing by quickly and the whole hour was about to be taken up in just singing.

As I began to steal quick glances at the congregation to see how they were reacting I noticed no one else seemed to be as uncomfortable as I was. In fact, they appeared happy and joyful as if they were having a good time.

So I figured if they did not mind singing so long they would not mind my preaching more than five or ten minutes.

However, I was very troubled and disturbed over the way they praised and worshipped. I had never seen, heard, or been at a service like that and it was a shock to me. When I got home that night I got out my concordance and found that the Bible actually listed numerous ways to praise the Lord. I also found that almost every book in the Bible mentioned different ways to worship and praise the Lord.

3. List the various forms of praise and worship described in Psalm 149:1–3 and Psalm 150:1–5.
   a. 149:1 _____
   b. 149:2 _____
   c. 149:3 _____
   d. 150:1 _____
   e. 150:2 _____
   f. 150:3 _____
   g. 150:4 _____
   h. 150:5 _____

4. What is the result of praise in Psalm 149:7–9?
   a. _____
   b. _____
   c. _____

5. For whom is this an honor? (Psalm 149:9) _____

The next night I decided that I would join in with their form of praise which everyone seemed to really enjoy. I did all right clapping my hands but the raising of hands troubled me. I managed to raise mine about chest high and felt so embarrassed I looked around to see who was watching. No one was looking. They were all too busy worshipping the Lord. A little later I was able to raise mine all the way to my shoulders and there they got stuck and just would not go any higher. I glanced at the man next to me. He had his eyes closed, hands above his head and a joyful smile on his face. I could hear him worshipping the Lord. With a determination to not miss out on the fun I said, "Jesus is Lord and I lift my hands unto Him"—and raised my hands above my head. In so doing, I experienced a tremendous release of my emotions. It felt really good.

6. What are we doing when we lift our hands? (Lamentations 3:41)

_____

7. What are some other reasons for the lifting up of hands?
   a. Lam. 2:19 _____
   b. I Tim. 2:8 _____
   c. Ps. 28:2 _____
   d. Ps. 63:4 _____
   e. Ps. 119:48 _____
   f. Ps. 141:2 _____

At another meeting, I got shocked again when the people began to Praise the Lord in the dance, not a worldly dancing, but one of dancing feet. Since, however, I had seen that it was scriptural, the shock was not as severe. But I still had trouble with this one for a couple of reasons. First of all it did not seem proper. Secondly, I was not a dancer. However, when I saw how some Christians danced with their feet it looked OK and I figured I could probably do it with a little practice. So, I practiced in my bedroom and discovered I not only could dance but it was really fun.

We saw in question three from Psalm 149:3 and Psalm 150:4 that dancing is a form of praising the Lord.

8. How did King David dance before the Lord? (2 Samuel 6:14) _____

_____

9. What does God turn mourning into? (Psalm 30:11) _____

10. Why? (Psalm 30:12) _____

_____

11. What happened in the Father's house when His lost son returned home? (Luke 15:25)

_____

The Results of Joy

In I Thessalonians 5:16–17, we are admonished to be joyful and give thanks in all things.

It is not surprising to find the enemy busy trying to keep the saints from emoting to God and entering into praise and worship with their total being. This is the way the enemy keeps us chained and defeated. Praise in the right way brings strength to God's people and releases the Spirit. In true praise we discover the truth of Nehemiah 8:10 ". . . for the joy of the Lord is your strength." True praise is more than just singing and reading the Word of God. Though there are certainly avenues to true praise and worship, there is much more. In true worship and praise, something transpires within our spirits that brings us into the presence of God—and we know we have come into His presence.

Enemies of Joy

From the following chart you will see the enemy uses depression, heaviness and grief to suppress joy and rob you of spiritual strength. However, it is possible to develop to a level of maturity in the Lord where you can even rejoice in the face of these circumstances. How you may experience victory will be shown for each area of warfare.

Questions to Stimulate Thought and Revelation from the Lord

12. What is joy and how is it different from happiness? _____
_____

13. Why do we have fullness of joy 24 hours a day? _____
_____

14. Why should Christians emote to God rather than ball games or other things of the world? _____

15. List six different ways we can praise the Lord.
    a. _____
    b. _____
    c. _____
    d. _____
    e. _____
    f. _____

Answers to Questions

1. Fullness of joy and pleasure evermore.

2. For God's pleasure.

3. a. 149:1 A new song.
   b. 149:2 Rejoice and be joyful.
   c. 149:3 Praise Him in the dance and with timbrel and harp.
   d. 150:1 Praise God in His sanctuary.
   e. 150:2 Praise Him for His mighty acts and according to His greatness.
   f. 150:3 Praise Him with trumpet, psaltery, harp.
   g. 150:4 Praise Him with timbrel and dance, stringed instruments and organs.
   h. 150:5 Praise Him upon loud cymbals and high sounding cymbals.

4. Bind their kings with chains, their nobles with iron fetters, and execute upon them the judgment written.

5. To all His saints.

6. We are lifting up our heart unto God.

7. a. Lam. 2:19 For the life of our young children
   b. I Tim. 2:8 Prayer
   c. Ps. 28:2 Supplication
   d. Ps. 63:4 Blessing the Lord
   e. Ps. 119:48 Unto His commandments
   f. Ps. 141:2 As a sacrifice

8. With all His might.

9. Dancing.

10. That my glory may sing praise to God and not be silent.

11. There was music and dancing.

12. Joy is a spiritual force and is independent of circumstances; happiness is an emotion or feeling dependent upon circumstances.

13. Because joy is in the presence of God and God is in us.

14. God is more deserving. Releases you into the spirit realm. Produces joy.

15. a. Singing
    b. Clapping
    c. Dancing
    d. Shouting
    e. Lifting hands
    f. Various musical instruments

WEAPON

JOY

TRAINING

**PRAISE
&
WORSHIP**

WARFARE

DEPRESSION   **HEAVINESS**   **GRIEF**
DESPAIR   GLOOM   MOURNING
DISCOURAGEMENT   BURDEN   SORROW
HOPELESSNESS   DISGUST   HEARTACHE
SUICIDE   SADNESS

VICTORY

STRENGTH

CHAPTER SEVEN: DEPRESSION

Despair Discouragement Hopelessness Suicide

Depression Defined

One of the weapons of the enemy to steal our joy is depression, which is an abnormal state of inactivity and unpleasant emotion. It is a dejection of mind, a lowering of the spirits as in sadness.

There are numerous situations and circumstances in life which create emotional stress and strain. The enemy uses these to wage war with the objective of taking away joy and of bringing people under the particular bondages of depression, heaviness, and grief.

The Results of Depression

If left unchecked, depression can lead into despair and discouragement which can develop into a sense of hopelessness. Once a state of hopelessness is reached it is easy to induce the thought of "why go on living" and thus open the victim up to committing suicide.

In our pressure-cooker society more and more people are being treated by doctors and psychologists for depression. Suicide is now the second leading cause of death among young people ages 15–24 years.

Women and Depression

Women, particularly housewives, appear to be more subject to depression than men. Perhaps this is because they toil day in and day out at washing dishes, cooking meals, caring for children, paying bills, running errands and maintaining a pace that would fatigue a man in a short period of time. Note: It is not the work that leads to depression but, rather, the work done with not so much as a thank you. Besides all of the family related activities, there are also social obligations which must somehow be squeezed into a hectic schedule. This is often done with little or no encouragement. As a result, depression, despair, discouragement, disinterest, distress, despondency and other emotional responses can be made.

Men and Depression

While women may get depressed over vague, generalized types of experiences, and may do so more often than men, it does not mean men are not subject to depression. For men it is usually more crisis-oriented such as a business setback, or illness. Many times a man finds himself too busy to take time with the kids or help the wife. He may be so caught up in his busy schedule and in his own problems that he does not become aware of the plight of his wife and children. He comes home to a lonely and often frustrated wife who has not had anyone she could talk and relate to for days—cleaning house, baby's mess, cooking and washing being the extent of her worth for several straight days. Because she gets little or no appreciation or encouragement, she feels very unworthy. She tries to communicate these things but he can't hear or understand. The stage is now set for both of them to be attacked by the enemy.

If they argue and fight, failing to realize they are in spiritual warfare, the door is opened wide for the enemy to destroy the marriage by bringing upon them various mental, emotional and physical illnesses, resulting in further depression.

How to Overcome Depression

The impact of depression can be minimized to a degree by the realization of the cyclical nature of emotions in both men and women. Experiences which create good feelings for a period of time are followed by lows or let down feelings. Depending upon personalities and temperaments, the peaks may have either a wide range of bounce or a narrow range. Some people receive good news about as calmly as they receive bad. Others get excited at ball games, while some never get too involved. There are still others who seem to go up and down like a roller coaster. One day everything makes them feel good and the next day nothing could make them feel good, not even news they just inherited a million dollars.

All of this adds up to the need for learning how to bring the emotions under the control of the spirit, clearly subjected to the Lordship of Jesus. Who wants to go through life being subjected to the whims of their emotions?

How to Overcome Despair

God did not design the Christian life to be lived under the domination of the soul, where emotions and the mind rule. He has given joy as a spiritual force to combat attitudes and remove roadblocks which keep one from living the abundant life Jesus gives. But joy is released only as one learns how to properly worship God—which is not an automatic accomplishment. Rather, it requires discipline of the soul. King David realized this as revealed in Psalm 42:11:
1. Who was David talking to? _____
2. What was the problem? _____
3. What was the root of the trouble? _____
4. What was the solution? _____

At the time David wrote this psalm he was in trouble and exiled from his throne. As he thought about the "good old days" he began to long for past experiences. In so doing, his emotions began to be subjected to warfare.
5. What did David start thinking in Psalm 42:3,9? _____

_____

6. What did he begin to remember? (Ps. 42:4) _____

_____

Thus we see David in a state of depression called despair as a result of his negative thinking.

7. What are we to discipline ourselves to think about? (Philippians 4:8)

a. _____ d. _____
b. _____ e. _____
c. _____ f. _____

This verse concludes, "if there is any excellence and if anything worthy of praise, let your mind dwell on these." In other words, if it will not produce praise do not let your mind dwell on it. This is very important due to the fact something may be true but not lovely. It may be right but not pure. The thought life must be guarded and disciplined to avoid dwelling upon circumstances which can be used to provoke one to despair. David realized that the way to overcome his depression was by using his weapon of joy through praise and worship.

How to Overcome Discouragement

The Apostle Paul had opportunities to battle against the weapon of discouragement. One account is recorded in Acts chapter 16. Paul and the men with him had gone into Macedonia as a result of his vision of a man asking them to come and help him. When they arrived they discovered a ladies prayer meeting and through their ministry a leading lady of the group was saved and she and her household were baptized. Furthermore she opened up her home for them to live in during their stay. For awhile everything was going fine and then the circumstances changed:

8. What did Paul do in Acts 16:16–18? _____

_____

9. How did her masters respond? (vs. 19–21) _____

_____

10. What happened to Paul and Silas? (vs. 22–24) _____

_____

In these circumstances, Paul and Silas had to make a decision as to what they would do. They were in warfare and everything in the natural was very discouraging. They were in a foreign land, locked in stocks in the deepest part of the prison. A natural form of attack from the enemy upon them would be to question why the other members of the group were not in the same fix—why us Lord? Silas would be open to the suggestion of his innocency. He had not done anything. It was Paul who cast the spirit out. And both would be subject to the hopelessness of their situation. Who could possibly do anything seeing that they were in a foreign prison with no rights. On top of all this there was the pain in their bodies from the beating and the discomfort of their feet being locked in stocks.

How long they were subjected to this form of attack or how close they came to losing the battle, the scripture does not reveal. However, they did not stay under their circumstance but began to wage war by using their weapon of joy through worship and praise.

11. What did Paul and Silas begin to do? (Acts 16:25) _____

_____

12. What were the results? (v. 26) _____

_____

A miracle was produced through Paul and Silas refusing to let their minds and emotions rule and becoming discouraged (which is the opposite of encouraged). The miraculous event that took place not only loosed Paul and Silas, it also broke the bonds holding the other prisoners and opened all the prison doors.

All this commotion awakened the jailer who, seeing the situation, immediately thought the prisoners had escaped. He knew he would be in disgrace and would face a fate worse than the prisoners. This immediately depressed him.

13. What did the jailer decide to do? (v. 27) _____
14. What kept him from committing suicide? (v. 28) _____

_____

The end result was salvation for the jailer and release for Paul and Silas. It appears that the jailer was the man that Paul had seen in the vision and that the circumstances which in the natural appeared to be a major defeat were used by God to produce victory.

15. What will God do with all circumstances for those trusting in Him? (Romans 8:28)

_____

How to Overcome Hopelessness

The enemy has a good reason for using his weapon of hopelessness to keep you from praising God.

When praises to God are going forth it releases one into the presence of God—while releasing the spiritual force joy to counter attack the mind and emotions. Joy and pleasure team up to give the believer encouragement instead of discouragement. They evoke hope instead of hopelessness, a desire to live rather than die.

16. According to Psalm 22:3, where does God live or inhabit? _____
17. What is in the presence of God and at His right hand? (Psalm 16:11)

_____

18. How do you enter into God's presence? (Psalm 100:4)
    a. _____
    b. _____
19. What are two things God gives in Romans 15:5?
    a. _____
    b. _____

From scriptures we see the importance of coming into God's presence when circumstances and our situation are creating negative thoughts and wrong emotional responses. He will give us a desire to persevere, to hang in there, to keep on trucking. He will show us it is not hopeless, that all things are possible. He will thus give us encouragement by assuring us that we are indeed going to make it. This prevents us from becoming discouraged and hopeless—which is a tell-tale sign one has not been in God's presence.

There is always something to be thankful for. No matter how bad the situation, it could always be worse. Someone once said "I was complaining about not having any shoes until I met a man who had no feet." Although it may be difficult to see something to be thankful for it is imperative to do so if we are to win the battle. As we begin to give thanks our mind and emotions are now receiving new commands. At first they may not want to respond: they would rather wallow in despair and discouragement and think of how hopeless everything is.

20. What command is given in Psalm 103:1–2? _____

_____

21. How is this command carried out in verse 2? _____

_____

22. What benefits are recalled in verses 3–5?
    a. _____ b. _____
    c. _____ d. _____
    e. _____ f. _____

Notice that the soul had to be commanded to bless the Lord. This is not a natural way of living. It is a spiritual way of living. But it also reveals that we can command our soul and make it subject to our spirit. In so doing we fulfill God's desire for us and our desire for enjoyment and pleasure—they are both in His presence. We are told in Revelation 4:11 (KJV) that the Lord is worthy to receive glory, and honor and power; that He created all things for His pleasure. In other words—God wants to enjoy us! We were created for this very purpose—His pleasure.

How can this be accomplished? First, become aware of why you were created. Second, desire to be a God-pleaser in every area of your life. Begin praying that you can be one who is a Father pleaser as was Jesus, who said, "And He who sent me is with me; He has not left me alone, for I always do the things that are pleasing to Him" (John 8:29).

It is true that each of us have different personalities and temperaments and thus will give God pleasure in different ways. However, we must all come into His presence in God's prescribed way. All arts require certain disciplines; basic principles must be understood, accepted and put into practice. Praise and worship are no exception.

Usually when we think of worship we think of singing, praising, and reading the Word of God. But in reality, these are merely avenues to true worship—for worship is much more than any of these expressions. In worship something transpires within the spirit that brings us into the presence of God—and we actually know whether or not we have come into His presence.

Suicide Defined

Suicide is self-murder. It is an act designed to destroy one's own life.

The Bible makes it very clear that the thief comes to steal, destroy and kill. He steals the Word of God out of people's heart, destroys their hope and, if left unchecked, he will kill them.

There are many causes of death; the most tragic is suicide. Here in America it is fast becoming the number one killer of youth, second only to auto accidents.

Causes of Suicide

One of the prime causes of suicide is despair of enslavement to sin. Drug addicts, alcoholics and homosexuals are prime candidates. They hurt on the inside and see how they

56

are hurting others. They think of how they are destroying their lives and become overwhelmed with guilt. Suicide seems to be the only way out.

Another cause of suicide among youth is a broken home. With more than a million new divorces each year, the thief has ample opportunity to victimize the children. Life appears hopeless and the urge to die is magnified.

Although not all children from broken homes are on the verge of suicide, many couples trace their marital problems back to their childhood years. They put up a good front for years and then the hurt, rejection, and hate explodes in many directions. Many times they begin to think of suicide; some commit suicide. Adversities in life can be used by the devil to make one believe all is lost and there is nothing left to live for.

23. How did Elijah respond to Jezebel's threat to kill him? (I Kgs. 19:4) _____
_____

24. Elijah thought he was the only one left serving God. How many people were still on God's side? (I Kgs. 19:18) _____

25. When disaster came to Job, what did he long for? (Job 3:21) _____

26. What was the actual outcome of his life?
    a. (Job 42:10) _____
    b. (Job 42:16) _____
    c. (Job 42:17) _____

27. What did Ahithophel do when his counsel to the king was not followed? (II Sam. 17:23)
_____

28. What did Zimri do when he saw the city was taken? (I Kgs. 16:18) _____
_____

Suicide is a very serious and dangerous game and not everyone who plays it wants to die. They just don't want to keep on living the way they are. However, the potential of going too far is in every suicide attempt.

Anyone playing the game is, in reality, crying out for help. Many times their loved ones and friends hear them make a comment about ending it all and think it is just talk. There is a need to recognize the danger of thinking and talking about suicide.

29. What is the purpose of such thoughts? (Rom. 7:23) _____

30. How does a person become what he is (Pro. 23:7) _____

31. What came upon Job? (Job 3:25) _____

Suicidal thoughts are seeds sown by the enemy. They are watered by loneliness and depression. Thoughts have a way of becoming words and words become deeds.

32. What power is in the tongue? (Pro. 18:21) _____

The power to live or die is in the tongue, because as one thinks, so he is, and so he will speak. One must not allow any thoughts of suicide to go unchallenged. Ask the Holy Spirit to help you. Fill your mind with the Word of God, not your circumstances.

The Greatest Deterrent to Suicide

The fear of God is the greatest deterrent to suicide. Because this generation is so trained in humanism they have trouble realizing there is truth and absolutes.

One absolute truth is that death is not an end but a beginning. Every person who commits suicide has sealed themselves to an eternity in hell.

Many have been deceived into thinking it is their life and their body and they have the right to do as they please. While they may do as they please, due to the fact they are a free mortal being, it is also true their body belongs to God. He is the Creator. He alone has the right to determine their destiny.

33. What does God command us to do with our bodies?
    a. (I Cor. 6:19,20) _____
    b. (I Ths. 5:23) _____
34. What will be the consequence of disobedience? (I Cor. 3:17) _____
35. What is the fear of the Lord? (Pro. 9:10) _____

Overcoming Suicide

The first step to victory is that of realizing you can help yourself. The book of Job is a good example of one who wanted to die, received a lot of counsel that in reality was of no help, and finally decided to do something. He decided to trust God.

Paul and Silas were in prison when an earthquake opened all the doors. The jailer was suddenly attacked by the thoughts of all the prisoners being gone and the disgrace it meant to him. He started to commit suicide. When Paul saw what he was about to do, he cried out "do yourself no harm; we are all still here" (Acts 16:28). The jailer then asked what he must do. They told him to trust God. "Believe on the Lord Jesus Christ, and thou shalt be saved" (Acts 16:31).

Simple, isn't it? Best of all is that it works. Job made it and so did the jailer. Defeat and failure were turned into a new life.

36. What is the first step in coming to God? (Heb. 11:6) _____
    _____
37. What did Job do after trusting God that turned his captivity? (Job 42:10) _____
    _____

Here we see the solution: Cry out to God and repent for not trusting Him and trying to justify yourself. Turn your hatred on your enemy who is trying to kill you. Take your eyes off yourself and forgive others. Then become concerned about their needs. Pray for them that God will bless and prosper them. Ask Him to allow you to help them in some way.

Remember, "for God so loved the world, that He gave His only begotten Son, that whosoever believeth in Him should not perish, but have everlasting life."

Questions to Stimulate Thought and Revelation from the Lord

38. What is depression? _____
39. How does the enemy subject people to depression, despair, discouragement, hopelessness and, finally, to suicide? _____
40. Did God design man to be under the domination of his spirit or of his soul? _____
    _____
41. What are the faculties of the soul which the enemy wages war against to keep one from coming into the presence of God? _____
42. Why are praise and worship important? _____
43. For what purpose was man created? _____

44. How can man accomplish this purpose? _____

45. What is the second killer of youth in America? _____

46. Name three causes of suicide

    a. _____

    b. _____

    c. _____

47. What is the greatest deterrent to suicide? _____

48. If you have been snared by depression, pray this prayer or one similar to it:

Father, I ask You to forgive me for allowing my emotions to rule my life, rather than Your Son, Jesus Christ. Forgive me for not trusting You and dwelling upon my circumstance. I now repent and refuse to walk in agreement with _____ (depression, despair, etc) and break its power, dominion and influence in my life through the name and blood of Jesus Christ. I ask the Holy Spirit to empower me to be a blessing to You. I command my soul to not forget all Your benefits which You have bestowed on me. In Jesus' Name, I pray. Amen.

Answers to Questions

1. His soul

2. His soul was in despair. He was discouraged

3. Lack of hope in God

4. Hope in God and praising Him

5. That God had forsaken him

6. God's faithfulness and loving kindness

7. a. true
   b. honest
   c. just
   d. pure
   e. lovely
   f. good report

8. Cast out a spirit of divination from a young girl

9. Seized them and brought them before the magistrates and accused them of teaching unlawful customs

10. They were beaten and cast into prison

11. Pray and sing praises unto God

12. There was an earthquake, doors were opened, everyone's bands were loosed

13. Kill himself

14. Paul showed concern and assured him everyone was still there

15. Work all things for the good

16. Praises of His people

17. Joy and pleasure

18. a. thanksgiving
    b. praise

19. a. patience
    b. consolation (encouragement)

20. Bless the Lord, oh my soul and all that is within me, bless His Holy Name

21. By not forgetting His benefits

22. a. forgives all my iniquities
    b. heals all my diseases
    c. redeemed my life from destruction
    d. crowned me with loving kindness and tender mercies
    e. satisfies my mouth with good things
    f. youth is renewed like the eagles

23. Ran away and requested that he might die

24. 7,000

25. Death

26. a. The Lord gave him twice as much as he had before
    b. lived 140 years and saw four generations
    c. died, being old and full of days

27. Hanged himself

28. Burnt his house over him and died

29. Bring into captivity to the law of sin

30. As he thinks in his heart, so he is

31. The thing he feared

32. Death and life

33. a. glorify God
    b. preserve blameless

34. Him shall God destroy

35. Beginning of Wisdom

36. Must believe that He is, and a rewarder of those who diligently seek Him

37. He prayed for his friends

38. Depression is an abnormal state of inactivity and unpleasant emotion, a dejection of mind, a lowering of the spirit as in sadness

39. Steals their job through various circumstances and situations which create emotional stress and strain

40. His spirit

41. Mind and emotions

42. Praise releases you into the presence of God. Worship releases the force of joy which counter attacks the mind and emotions. Joy gives encouragement instead of discouragement. Hope instead of hopelessness. A desire to live, rather than die

43. For God's pleasure

44. First, become aware of why you were created. Second, desire to be a God pleaser in every area of your life

45. Suicide

46. a. despair of enslavement to sin
    b. life appears hopeless
    c. adversities

47. Fear of God

CHAPTER EIGHT: HEAVINESS

Gloom   Burden   Disgust

Heaviness Defined

The chart on page 51 shows "heaviness" as another weapon used by the enemy to try to steal our joy. My dictionary describes heaviness as "not easy to bear; burdensome; oppressive; afflictive." It further describes one with heaviness as being "bowed down with care, slow or dull; sluggish; lacking mirth or gaiety. Gloomy, overcast, and overcome with weariness."

The Nature of Heaviness

I would venture to say every christian has experienced heaviness in some manner or another. For in each of our lives there comes trials and tribulations as a natural result of the world we live in—a world at enmity with God. There are, of course, those trials we bring upon ourselves through sin and ignorance. Then there are those tests and trials which God initiates.

Regardless of the nature or origin, one thing is for certain—the enemy will wage war against us to use circumstances in any way he can to get us to feel heaviness, gloominess, disgust, or the feeling that the circumstance is just too much of a burden to bear.

How to Overcome Heaviness

Sometimes we find ourselves low in spirit for no apparent reason. As we learned from our study on depression, this is because our emotions are subjective and objective.

David was one who went from high to low emotional states as seen in the Psalms. One moment he was in great despair and was not even sure if dying would make him feel better and the next he would be soaring up into the heavenlies declaring the goodness of God. At times he cried out "My God why hast thou forsaken me?" (Psalm 22:1). At other times he would say, "My soul waits in silence for God only: from Him is my salvation. He only is my rock and my salvation, my stronghold, I shall not be greatly shaken" (Psalm 62:1).

There were other men in the Bible who also had their times of heaviness. For example, the apostle Paul wrote the following to the saints at Corinth: (II Corinthians 2:8–10)

> For we do not want you to be unaware, brethren, of our affliction which came to us in Asia, that we were burdened excessively beyond our strength, so that we despaired even of life; indeed, we had the sentence of death within ourselves in order that we should not trust in

ourselves, but in God who raises the dead; who delivered us from so great a peril of death, and will deliver us, He on whom we have set our hope, and He will yet deliver us.

It was this same Paul who also was caught up to the third heaven and heard things from God he was not able to share with others (2 Corinthians 12:2–4).

How to Avoid Burdens

There are many other examples in the Bible, which show that from the highest to the lowest, greatest to the least, God's people go through difficult times. Therefore, the question is not will we have difficult times, or even why do we have tests and trials, but rather how will we handle them and what will they accomplish in our life.

1. What can one expect in the world? (John 16:33) _____

The word tribulation is the same word used for pressing out grapes in the wine press. From that sense the verse reveals that in the world is constant pressure. It concludes with a reassuring note, ". . . but take courage; I have overcome the world."

We find this also expressed in Psalm 34:19–20 (KJ) "Many are the afflictions of the righteous: BUT the Lord delivers him of them all. He keeps all his bones: not one of them is broken.

It is important to notice the colon in the sentence structure, it means an explanation is coming. Next, notice the word BUT. If you overlook these, you will miss the whole meaning of what the scripture is teaching.

Many people stop before the BUT; in the world we shall have tribulation; many are the afflictions of the righteous. They stop and begin to tribulate and suffer afflictions for the Lord. In so doing, they become snared with heaviness.

Yes, it is true that in the world we shall have tribulation, BUT be of good courage, I have overcome the world. In other words, don't lose your joy!

Yes, it is true that many are the afflictions of the righteous, BUT the Lord delivers him of them all.

These scriptures are proclaiming good news. In the midst of the pressures of the world we can be of good courage because we know our Lord shall deliver us. Therefore, we maintain our joy and avoid the snare of heaviness.

One way we are assured of being delivered is from the lives of men in the Bible; because God never changes, the Bible is relevant to us today. Therefore, He will deal with us today just as He did with Abraham, Moses, Paul and others. So, as we read of His justice, mercy, faithfulness, goodness and compassion in seeing them through their hassles, tests, trials, tribulations and pressures we can be assured He will do the same for us. We take courage in the fact that He who overcame the world now lives right inside of us to accomplish the same victory in our lives—to establish the kingdom of God within us.

2. What is the kingdom of God *not* and what *is* it? (Romans 14:17)

    a. _____

    b. _____

3. Where is the kingdom of God? (Luke 17:20–21) _____

It is imperative to know and understand that the kingdom of God is different than the world. In the world there are tests, trials, tribulations, pressure which can be so heavy that we respond with gloom, burden or disgust. But the Bible tells us that the kingdom of God is righteousness, peace and joy in the Holy Spirit. But how can this be, one may ask? How can I have joy when everything is being shaken?

4. How is the kingdom to be established within?
   a. (Luke 22:28–30) _____
   b. (Acts 14:22) _____

Thus, we discover that circumstances are God's way of training us for kingdom living. He dealt the same way with Jesus: "although He was a Son, He learned obedience from the things which He suffered." (Hebrews 5:8)

In the preceding verse we are told that Jesus prayed with loud crying and tears. Tests and trials are not always easy to bear, yet they can be borne.

5. God will not let us be tested beyond what point? (I Corinthians 10:13)

   _____

6. What kind of test and trials will we face? (I Corinthians 10:13) _____

   _____

7. What will God do with the test? (I Corinthians 10:13) _____

   _____

8. How should one respond to test?
   a. (James 1:2) _____
   b. (I Thessalonians 5:18) _____
9. What does testing produce? (James 1:3) _____
10. What is the end result?
    a. (James 1:4) _____
    b. (James 1:12) _____
11. How long will a test or trial last? (I Peter 1:6) _____

Here we have read some encouraging scripture. God is faithful and will not allow us to be placed in a circumstance that we can not handle. However, the enemy will be quick to suggest we can not bear the load—that we are going to be crushed. He will wage all-out war to magnify and exalt the problem in order to keep our eyes off Jesus who is our strength and help. If he is successful this will prevent our hearts from being able to praise and release joy as a weapon to win over our test and trials.

These scriptures reveal truth that sets us free: our situation is not weird or extraordinary; we haven't been singled out for special treatment; it is a common experience. Others have been through or may be going through similar circumstances. Another thought conveyed by scripture is that it will be in the natural and physical—common to man.

We are further told God will show the way out. The way out is not necessarily away from the difficulty. Sometimes it may be enduring and going through it, coming out undaunted on the other side. My personal experiences and observations have taught me that one usually must go through to the other side. Although it is always suggested by the enemy that the way out is to change the circumstance, it is a rare exception when a problem is solved in this manner (i.e., trouble with your boss means you should quit and find another job).

Finally, we read what is perhaps the best news of all: our tests and trials will come to an end. They are not forever. The tests are only for a little while, just for a season. Then it is all over. Sometimes it may seem as though things will never get better, as did one fellow who came up with this little poem I read somewhere:

one day as I set sad and alone
musing about the things I had done
and how bad things were going
a voice came to me and said,
"cheer up, things could be worse."
so I cheered up
and sure enough, things got worse.

Going through a test or trial can be made easier by using joy as a spiritual force to counter the feeling of heaviness. When all looks so gloomy and the burden seems too heavy to bear or when you've done everything you know how to do and the feeling of heaviness or disgust begins to creep in, put off these attacks of the enemy by beginning to rejoice and counting it all joy and putting on the garment of praise (Isaiah 61:3).

Test and trials can cause you to become disgusted. When this happens, the pressure to quit becomes intense. "Oh what's the use of trying anymore" is a common response. However, as God's people, we cannot quit. We may feel like it and may even say it. I have said it a few times myself. But there is no turning back. If Jesus is not the way, what is? And love never fails. So we don't quit. We worship and praise to release joy—which is our strength.

Remember that God's objective is to establish His kingdom within. The pressures of life are designed to make us turn *to* Him, not *away from* Him. Jesus said "to take courage" not to run away or quit.

How to Overcome Disgust and the Urge to Quit

God is so good to us and loves us so much that even if we do try to run away and quit He will never leave us or forsake us. How do we know that? By the way He responded to the prophet Elijah. This great man of God challenged 450 false prophets of Baal on Mt. Carmel and saw fire come down and consume his offering and altar which had been soaked in water and also licked up the water on the ground. Yet, when he heard king Ahab's wife Jezebel say she was going to have him killed because of what God had done through him he quit and started running. He was running for his life, not realizing that he was running away from God's purposes. He stopped running when he got to the wilderness, and there, full of self-pity, disgusted with the results of his obedience to God, he began to lament and requested that he might die. Instead of God becoming angry and wrathful He sent an angel to feed him a couple of meals to strengthen him. God then sent Elijah to return and face his circumstances. He had to deal with king Ahab and Jezebel. The next thing is that he won, they lost.

12. What does God give to the believer instead of a spirit of heaviness or fainting? (Isaiah 61:3) _____

13. For what purpose will God make everything work toward if we allow Him to? (Romans 8:28) _____

14. What then should we say about our circumstance? (Romans 8:31)
_____

15. List all the things which can not separate us from the Love of God. (Romans 8:35–39)
    a. _____ b. _____ c. _____
    d. _____ e. _____ f. _____

g. _____ h. _____ i. _____
j. _____ k. _____ l. _____
m. _____ n. _____ o. _____
p. _____ q. _____

16. How often should a Christian rejoice? (I Thessalonians 5:16) _____
_____

17. How should a Christian pray? (I Thessalonians 5:17) _____
_____

18. In what should a Christian give thanks? (I Thessalonians 5:18) _____
_____

19. Why should he give thanks? (I Thessalonians 5:18) _____
_____

20. If you do not give thanks what is the result? (I Thessalonians 5:19) _____
_____

21. How do you enter into the gates and court of God? (Psalm 100:4)
    a. _____
    b. _____

22. What is in the presence of God and at His right hand? (Psalm 16:11)
    a. _____
    b. _____

Notice that in verse 39 it is written ". . . from the love of God which is in Christ Jesus our Lord." Thus it is evident why we must run to Jesus and not away from Him, why we must become Jesus centered and not problem centered.

Knowing that these things are not able to separate us from God's love enables us to use our weapon of joy by releasing praise and worship to Him no matter what the circumstances may be. As we are able to do this we discover the truth of Nehemiah 8:10, ". . . for the joy of the Lord is your strength."

The first attempt to rejoice and give thanks in an adverse situation may not be too successful The mind and emotions will not automatically cooperate. Why should I give thanks for this, is a natural response. This is actually a slight twist of the scripture. God did not say give thanks *for* but give thanks *in* everything. Why? Because He knows how to deliver the righteous. As it is written, "the Lord knows how to rescue the Godly from temptation, and to keep the unrighteous under punishment for the day of judgment" (II Peter 2:9). And again in Psalm 34:17–19, "The righteous cry and the Lord hears, and delivers them out of all their troubles. The Lord is near to the broken hearted, and saves those who are crushed in spirit. Many are the afflictions of the righteous, but the Lord delivers him out of them all."

No wonder the enemy attempts to bring heaviness, gloom or burden upon one going through a test or trial. In so doing he keeps the weapon of joy from being used to bring forth praise, thanks and worship. This keeps the believer from coming into the presence of God where he will find strength, encouragement and the way out.

How to Evaluate Your Circumstances

God is for us, wanting us to be made whole and complete, lacking nothing. Desiring the establishing of His kingdom within, it is necessary to evaluate what is going on from a perspective of what is God after. What is to be the proper response?

Sometimes adverse circumstances are self-created. Galatians 6:7 states "whatever you sow, you will also reap." We need to be honest with God and ourselves at all times. If the circumstance is a result of sin, poor judgment, wrong attitude or due to our personality and temperament—we need to admit it. Then we should take steps to correct the cause. These types of lessons can teach us how to avoid similar circumstances later.

There are times when God may use circumstances to direct us toward another work, ministry or location. This needs to be ascertained through evaluation.

I know a college basketball coach who went through some trying ordeals which led to his resigning, moving to a new location and a different type of work which eventually led him into full time Christian ministry. He is now a very fulfilled person.

The following evaluation guideline can help you think through your situation:

1) Write down some specific yet simple details of your situation.

2) Recall how it all got started. You may see a critical incident at which things began to turn from good to bad.

3) Evaluate your role. Do you have a clean heart and clean hands. Be brutally honest. If you were wrong in any manner you need to confess it to God and receive forgiveness. If God so directs you may need to go and confess your wrong to others involved and ask their forgiveness.

4) What has been the effect with regard to:
   —your spiritual life: reading the Bible, prayer, fellowship with God and other believers, and sharing of your faith?
   —your family: wife, children, relatives?

If the circumstances have affected you in these areas you cannot allow them to go uncorrected. For the sake of your own well being and others, action must be taken.

5) What have you learned so far from your experience?

6) What is God trying to teach you? For example: If you are having conflict with your boss, pastor or some other leader God may be trying to show you have a problem with rebellion and independence. He may have decided it is time for you to learn Biblical submission and authority.

Conflict in the home with wife or children, may indicate God wants to teach you His Way with regard to marriage and being a parent.

If you are without a job or having financial problems God may be teaching you to depend upon Him or to be a good steward of your money.

If you are being treated unjustly or unfairly God may be teaching you how to have peace and refrain from vengeance.

If you have tried everything you know to be spiritual, to change the situation and nothing appears to be happening, He may be teaching you something about perseverence.

7) If you changed the circumstances would you miss a lesson from God?

8) What are some possible solutions? Prayer, counsel from a more mature, solid, Godly person.

9) What action can you take now?

It appears to me we need a breakthrough in how to handle our trials and afflictions.

We need to stop being downtrodden by the enemy. And we also need to stop avoiding the lessons that God is trying to teach us.

Learning how to rejoice and give thanks is not the total answer, but it is a beginning.

Questions to Stimulate Thought and Revelation from the Lord

23. Why do Christians have test, trials, tribulation and afflictions? _____
_____

24. How does the kingdom of God differ from the world? _____
_____

25. What type of warfare can you expect during adverse circumstances? _____

26. Why is God good to allow these to happen? _____
_____

27. What makes the Bible relevant to us today? _____

28. How will God deal with us in our situation? _____

29. Do the guidlines evaluation for yourself.

30. If you are experiencing heaviness and/or it's accompanying companions, pray this prayer or one similar to it:

> Father, I thank You for revealing to me that my situation and circumstance is subject to change. Forgive me for not trusting You and allowing my emotions to rule instead of Jesus. In the Name of Jesus, I take authority over this _____
> (name what it is—heaviness, disgust, etc.) and break its power, dominion and influence in my life. I now release the fruit of joy to flood my soul and place upon my soul the garment of praise. Thank you for releasing me in Jesus' Name, I pray. Amen.

Answers to Questions

1. Tribulation
2. a. It is not eating and drinking
   b. it is righteousness, peace, and joy in the Holy Ghost
3. Within you
4. a. Continuing with Jesus and in the faith
   b. through tests and tribulations
5. That you are able
6. Common to man
7. Make a way to escape
8. a. consider it all joy
   b. in everything give thanks
9. Patience
10. a. perfect, entire, wanting nothing
    b. receive the crown of life
11. For a season
12. Garment of praise
13. Good
14. If God is for us, who can be against us
15. a. tribulation
    b. distress
    c. persecution
    d. famine
    e. nakedness
    f. peril
    g. sword
    h. death
    i. life
    j. angels
    k. principalities
    l. powers
    m. things present
    n. things to come
    o. height
    p. depth
    q. creature
16. Rejoice evermore
17. Without ceasing
18. Everything
19. For this is the will of God
20. Quench the Spirit
21. a. thanksgiving
    b. praise
22. a. joy
    b. pleasure

23. Because our emotions are subjective and not objective, and we live in a world at enmity with God.
24. In the world are tests, trials, tribulations and various pressures; in the kingdom of God is righteousness, peace, joy in the Holy Spirit.
25. The type to get us to feel heaviness, gloominess, disgust, or that the circumstance is just too much of a burden to bear.
26. He wants us to be made whole and complete, lacking nothing.
27. God never changes. His Word is the same today as yesterday.
28. In the same manner of justice, mercy, faithfulness, goodness and compassion as He dealt with people in the Bible.

CHAPTER NINE: GRIEF

Mourning   Sorrow   Heartache   Sadness

Grief Defined

The third weapon the enemy uses to steal our joy is grief: the pain of mind produced by loss, misfortune, injury or evils of any kind. We are especially vulnerable to this in times of sorrow, heartache or sadness. There is a Godly sorrow and sadness. But there is also an ungodly one. We need to know the difference between the two.

Overcoming Grief

I was visiting a church when a lady came forward for ministry. She talked for a few minutes with the pastor who asked me if I would minister to her. She told me that in recent weeks there had been several deaths in her family, including a recent suicide. She was unable to cope with all the strain and found herself crying most of the time and unable to function normally. As she was explaining her problems, the Holy Spirit was speaking to me that I was being confronted with a spirit of grief. I silently asked Him how I was to minister to her. He replied that I was to bind up and cast out the spirit of grief and release joy upon her. I laid my hands upon her and ministered as directed. When I released joy upon her, she immediately fell to the floor and began to laugh joyfully. I saw her again several months later and she told me that after I prayed for her she found an indescribable joy and instead of crying, she laughed a lot for the next two or three days. After that, she found that because she was able to enter into praise and worship that her grief was gone.

How to Overcome Sorrow

Some of the sorrows of life are natural and some are caused by the god of this world.
1. What did Jesus say about sorrow? (John 16:20) _____
_____

2. What did the Apostle Paul say about grief, and what it resulted from?
   (I Thessalonians 4:13) _____
_____

Jesus was correct when He told the disciples they would be sorrowful. They sorrowed because something unforeseen happened and they were not prepared for it. They were planning on building a kingdom only to find their King nailed to a cross. When this happened, they locked themselves in behind closed doors and the world out. But then

69

something else happened which turned their sorrow into joy. It was something Jesus had told them many times would happen, but somehow they missed it—He arose from the dead. This revived their faith and confidence. Now they could once again praise and worship God. In so doing, they released their joy and overcame their grief, mourning, sorrow, heartache and sadness.

This event means something to us. It means that we may sorrow but not without hope. Jesus makes the difference. Because He lives, our sorrow is not of the world but it is a godly sorrow. It not only means we can fellowship with His sufferings, but also with His resurrection. Therefore, our sorrow is beautifully mixed with love, joy, peace and the wonderful presence of God.

Understanding Death

Our cruel enemy attempts to take the death of a loved one, be it family, relative, friend or acquaintance, and use it as a means of robbing us of our joy and robbing God of His praise and worship.

But God has given to us joy and the devil can not take it away as long as we keep our hope fixed on Jesus Christ. It is Christ in us the hope of glory (Col. 1:27)

Christians need teaching on death and the victory it brings. This would take away most of the tactics used by the enemy to bring people under the bondage of grief, mourning, heartache and sadness over the death of a loved one.

3. What truth about living and dying is revealed in Romans 14:7–9?
   a. _____
   b. _____
   c. _____

It was this knowledge which sustained the heroes of faith recorded in the scriptures. They knew there was a crown laid up for them, and that even in dying, they had victory. This allowed them to release joy in the midst of trials and tribulations and to sing when being put to death. This same truth allows Christians today to be the happiest people on earth in every circumstance and situation.

So we take our weapon of joy through releasing praise and worship to our king, creator, life and victor, knowing that even in death He defeats the enemy and receives glory and honor. Therefore, joy and life are made possible.

There are three types of death listed in the scripture. The first one is described above and refers to the spiritual realm. We die to self and live to Christ. The wages of sin is death we are told in Romans 6:23, but the gift of God is eternal life in Christ Jesus. Spiritual death is similar to being denied the rights and privileges as a citizen of your country. Sin, which causes spiritual death, keeps us from exercising the rights and privileges as a citizen in the kingdom of God. The word "death" or "dead" in the Greek language means to make inactive, inoperative, to deprive of power, to render weak and impotent.

The second type of death is the one most people think of—physical death. "The wages of sin is death"—not only spiritually but also physically. In this second type of death the spirit of man leaves his body. Consequently the body has no more function since its purpose is to carry our spirit around planet earth. The body thus returns to dust from whence it came.

4. The spirit did not come from dust. Where did it come from? (Genesis 2:7 and Zechariah 12:1) _____

_____

What happens to the spirit at death is a question most people had rather not think about. However, if one knows the answer and is assured in his heart that he has eternal life, death is no big deal; just a means of starting a new way of living in a new dimension.

The third type of death mentioned in the scripture is called the "second death" (Revelation 20:6,14). We are told that this third type of death is eternal separation from God by being thrown into the lake of fire with the devil, the beast and the false prophet (Revelation 20:10,15). This will happen to anyone whose name is not found written in the book of life.

How to Overcome the Fear of Death

We found in our study of fear that the devil is always trying to give us fear images. The ultimate torment of fear will be the fear of dying, the fear of perishing.
5. Why do we not have to fear death?
   a. Romans 6:6–11 _____
   b. Hebrews 2:14–15 _____
   c. I John 5:13 _____
6. What happens when a believer dies physically?
   a. II Corinthians 5:1,8 _____
   b. Ecclesiastes 12:7 _____
   c. Isaiah 57:1–2 _____
   d. Revelations 14:13 _____

Now perhaps we can get a glimpse of why Paul wrote in Philippians 1:21 "For me to live is Christ, and to die is gain." He was not uninformed of the blessing death brings. He viewed it as victory in I Corinthians 15:55–57. After all, what could be greater than being home with our Lord? Many Christians need to renew their minds with the truths in the Scriptures concerning death and dying.

Absent from the body means to be present with our Lord (Philippians 1:23–24). Although heaven is not God's ultimate goal for us—it is for us to be like Jesus and get heaven on earth—He has prepared a place of rest for those who die before Jesus returns (John 14:1–3).

The Meaning of Resurrection

Those in heaven are awaiting the resurrection which is not an event but a person. Jesus said it this way in John 11:25–26 (NAS) "I am the resurrection and the life; he who believes in Me shall live even if he dies, and everyone who lives and believes in Me shall never die. Do you believe this?" If our answer to His question is yes, then we are free from the fear of death for ourselves and our loved ones. We can rejoice and give praise even in death—which releases joy and delivers us from a worldly grief.
7. But how are our bodies resurrected?
   a. Philippians 3:20–21 _____

b. I Corinthians 15:50–54 _____

c. II Corinthians 5:4 _____

True resurrection is when our life is completely swallowed up in Jesus, who is life. Therefore, whatever has been missed through prayers, laying on of hands, anointing with oil, doctors, medicine or any other effort will be corrected and made perfect through death. Then shall come to pass the saying that death is swallowed up in victory.

There will be no sickness, disease, lame, crippled or deformed believers when they are swallowed up in Jesus. Yes, we may have sorrow over the death of a loved one, but the joy of knowing the victory produces in us a strength that passes understanding. Therefore, our sorrow and mourning is taken away and instead of grief there is praise and worship.

Through training in praise and worship we develop skill in using the weapon of joy to overcome the evil one. We obtain the victory which is strength in any circumstance or situation. Depression, heaviness and grief are all sent far from us—and are kept away from us as we stand firm in Jesus Christ, releasing joy in our whole being as we render praise and worship to the Lord of Lords and King of Kings—and "the joy of the Lord is our strength."

Questions to Stimulate Thought and Revelation from the Lord

8. What does the Spirit of God give in place of mourning or fainting (heaviness in KJV) (Isaiah 61:3) _____
_____

9. What are the results? _____
_____

10. Why were the disciples sorrowful over Jesus' death? _____
_____

11. What caused their sorrow to turn into joy? _____

12. What knowledge sustained the heroes of faith and other Christians and allowed them to be joyful even while being put to death? _____
_____

13. What is the resurrection? _____
_____

14. If you have been overtaken with grief, mourning, heartache, or sadness, obtain your release by saying this or a similar prayer:

> Father, I see that by being uninformed and not keeping my eyes fixed on You I have allowed a spirit of _____ (name the spirit) to influence my life and bring me into bondage. I now repent of this and turn from it. In the name of Jesus I command the spirit of _____ to depart. I break its power, dominion and influence in my life and in its place I receive the oil of gladness and the spirit of praise. I now release joy into my soul that You may be glorified." In Jesus' Name I pray. Amen.

Answers to Questions

1. Shall be turned to Joy

2. Ignorance and having no hope produces grief

3. a. no one lives or dies to himself
   b. we live and die unto the Lord, who is
   c. Lord of both the dead and living

4. God

5. a. Jesus died for us
   b. Jesus render the devil powerless
   c. we have eternal life

6. a. absent from the body, home with the Lord
   b. spirit returns to the Lord
   c. taken away from the evil to come
   d. enters into peace, is blessed, and obtains rest from labors

7. a. changed in the twinkling of an eye. Perishable puts on impershable and mortal puts on immortality
   b. receives a glorious body, like Jesus
   c. swallowed up by life

8. Oil of joy for mourning. Garment of praise for heaviness

9. Will be called trees of righteousness, the planting of the Lord that He might be glorified

10. It was unforeseen and they were not prepared for it

11. He arose from the dead

12. They knew there was a crown laid up for them, and that in dying they had victory

13. A person—Jesus Christ

CHAPTER TEN: PEACE

Peace Defined

Peace is a state of quiet or tranquility, freedom from disturbance or agitation. It is one of the most elusive conditions to man—but universally sought after. Furthermore, peace is also a very effective weapon to use in waging spiritual warfare. In fact, it is so effective and important that without it, life cannot be blessed and abundant.

The Concern for Peace of Mind

Peace, especially peace of the mind, is a growing concern for a vast number of people in all walks of life. There is hardly a person, young or old, male or female, single or married that is not under some type of stress, whether it comes from a job, inflation, the home, or world conditions. This means no one is immune to ample opportunities for worry, anxiety, fear, tension, distress and a host of similar maladies. The increase in sales of drugs to aid people under these stresses and the increase of patients in mental hospitals and/or under doctors' care clearly tell us that the enemy is waging a fairly successful war.

As we learned in our previous lesson, in the world we will face adverse circumstances and situations, we will have test and trials. Therefore, it is of utmost importance that we learn how to use our weapon of peace effectively. Only the Lord Jesus can keep us in "perfect peace;" therefore, we need to know what the Bible tells us about peace and how we can have the "peace that passes all understanding."

Jesus spoke about world conditions in the last days and the effects it would have on some people in Luke 21:25-26.

1. How did Jesus say some would respond to what they saw and heard about world conditions? _____

Some Worldly Methods to Produce Peace

I recently saw an advertisement in a newspaper urging people to become students of a mind control school in order to have control over health, memory, creativity, fears, weight, smoking, sleep, motivation, concentration and other problems (about the only claim not made was to grow hair).

It seems that almost everywhere you look, whether in newspapers, magazines, books, in the schools, adult classes, YMCA and even at the local church, someone is promoting and praising the virtue of meditation, hypnosis, yoga or some other means of producing peace.

The idea of being able to escape the strains of life is appealing to everyone. Because some clergy, respected businessmen, sport or movie celebrities say the above is good and works, many people think it must be O.K. We therefore see more and more unsuspecting, innocent people being seduced into paying their hard earned money into the hands of people who are not able to give peace. Jesus is called the Prince of Peace and He only can give peace.

Not only has the enemy manipulated his subjects to produce the conditions creating all the stress, he has been quick to introduce a host of eastern mystical religions and philosophies as a purported means of overcoming the stress. In reality they create a more severe stress as is testified by many who have been ripped off by them.

For example, one form of meditation involves repeating a mantra (the name of a demon) as a means of emptying the mind and thus relaxing the automatic nervous system. Those who have so experimented and found some type of relief also found themselves going deeper and deeper into this modern version of vedantic spirituality. As they released more and more of themselves to the demon(s), they discovered that instead of becoming free from stress they were actually unable to break loose from the demonic forces which took control of their mind. Fortunately, they were able to obtain help and, through the power of Jesus, were set free. The experiences of these and many others confirm that the only way to peace is through the Prince of Peace—Jesus.

How to Obtain Peace

The Lord neither advocates or exercises mind control. He does not violate man's free will and his ability to make decisions. Instead He teaches us how we may develop the fruit of peace and overcome the weapons of the enemy and experience "the peace that passes all understanding."

2. Who are the ones that have great peace? (Psalm 119:165)

_____

3. What is the further result of God's law? _____

_____

It is obvious from observing people involved in the previously mentioned methods of mysticism or those taking pills or booze that they have not found the answer of how to obtain peace.

4. Who does God keep in perfect peace? (Isaiah 26:3) _____

_____

5. Why? _____

Rather than putting our trust in the devices of the world we need to put our trust in God. When we do, we find He keeps us in perfect peace. It is difficult to trust someone we do not know. We might loan a hundred dollars to someone we knew would pay us back. However, we would probably not loan money to a stranger. Thus we see why many people are unable to trust God, love His law, and keep their mind on Him: because they really do not know Him. They may know about Him, but they do not know Him. It is easy to trust God if we know Him. In fact, He is the most trustworthy Being in the whole universe!

6. Why should you not put your trust in man? (Je. 17:5–6)
   a. _____
   b. _____

c. _____

d. _____

7. Why should you put your trust in God? (Je. 17:7–8)

   a. _____

   b. _____

   c. _____

   d. _____

   e. _____

   f. _____

8. What were the people in Isaiah 47:8–15 trusting in?

   a. _____

   b. _____

   c. _____

9. What were the results in verses 9, 11, 15?

   a. v. 9 _____

   b. v. 9 _____

   c. v. 11 _____

   d. v. 11 _____

   e. v. 11 _____

   f. v. 12 _____

10. For what purpose does God teach us and how does He lead us? (Isaiah 48:17)

   a. _____

   b. _____

11. If we pay attention and obey what will be the result? (Isaiah 48:18 KJ)

   a. _____

   b. _____

We are in spiritual warfare. All is fair to our enemy in this battle for control of man. He is aware of a profound truth in Proverbs 23:7—"For as he thinks within himself, so he is. . ." Therefore, if anyone can control the mind he can control the man. This will be brought to light further when we study the fruit of temperance and its effect upon the mind.

Two Kinds of Peace

At this point we need to reflect upon the truth that there are two kinds of peace: one which the world offers and one which Jesus offers. Each requires the seeker to commit himself and to discipline himself. One is everlasting, the other leads eventually to further stress.

12. What claims about peace does Jesus make in John 14:27? _____

13. What does the Lord give and bless His people with? (Psalm 29:11)

   a. _____

   b. _____

14. What does the world give us? (John 16:33) _____

15. What has Jesus done to encourage us? (John 16:33) _____

We see from these scriptures that the world's claim to give us peace is false. There is only one way to have peace and that is in Jesus, the Prince of Peace.

Since God teaches us for our profit, if we pay attention, our peace will be like a river. Therefore, as we look at how peace overcomes the weapons of our enemy and begin to practice God's way, we shall learn how to have freedom from Satan's devices and instead have perfect peace.

If you have been deeply involved in any of the eastern religions it would be advisable to obtain counsel from a mature, experienced Christian.

The chart following demonstrates the warfare waged against us to rob us of our peace.

Questions to Stimulate Thought and Revelation from the Lord

16. What are some conditions in the world which rob people of their peace? _____
_____

17. What is going to happen in the world as this age comes to an end? _____
_____

18. Name some ways the world offers to give peace: _____
_____

19. What is the end result of these ways? _____
_____

20. Does God advocate mind control? Why? _____

21. How does it become easy to trust God? _____

22. If you have been trusting in the world's way of obtaining peace rather than trusting God and desire to make a change and be set free from the snare of the enemy you may do so by praying this or a similar prayer:

"Father I have sinned against you by trusting in the world's methods rather than You for peace. I ask you to forgive me and renounce my trust in _____
(name what you have been trusting). In the name of Jesus I take authority over the spirits of _____ (meditation, yoga, etc.) and break their power and influence in my life and command them to leave. I now put my trust in Jesus who is my Lord and my Peace."

Answers to Questions

1. Hearts would fail them
2. They that love God's law
3. Nothing shall offend them
4. The one whose mind is stayed on Him
5. Because he trusts in the Lord
6. a. cursed
   b. like a bush in the desert
   c. will not see when prosperity comes
   d. live in stony wastes in the wilderness
7. a. blessed
   b. be like a tree planted by the water
   c. will not fear when the heat comes
   d. leaves will be green
   e. not anxious in year of drought
   f. not cease to yield fruit
8. Their wickedness; astrologers; star-gazers; monthly prognosticators
9. a. loss of children
   b. widowhood
   c. evil
   d. mischief
   e. desolation
   f. none shall save thee
10. a. to profit
    b. leads in the way you should go
11. a. peace as a river
    b. righteousness as the waves of the sea
12. That He gives peace, but not as the world
13. a. strength
    b. peace
14. Tribulation—test and trials
15. Overcome the world
16. Job, inflation, home conditions, world conditions
17. Things are going to get worse
18. Meditation, hypnosis, yoga
19. Mind control
20. Because He will not violate man's free will
21. By getting to know Him

WEAPON

PEACE

TRAINING

**MIND ON
JESUS**

WARFARE

WORRY
CARES
ANXIETY

NERVOUSNESS
TENSION
HEADACHE
NERVOUS
 HABITS
RESTLESSNESS
STRESS

DREAD
APPREHENSION
TERROR
FEAR
DISTRESS

VICTORY

FREEDOM

CHAPTER ELEVEN: WORRY

Worry   Anxiety   Cares

Worry Defined

From the chart on page 80 we learn that one weapon the enemy uses to steal and destroy peace is worry. To worry means to tease, to trouble, to harass with importunity or with care and anxiety.

In our society there is ample opportunity for the enemy to engage us in this spiritual warfare: getting married, raising children, obtaining an education, finding employment, buying a house, paying bills and many other circumstances make us vulnerable to worry.

Each of us has the ability to worry about anything or nothing. We can worry day or night, anytime, and in any place. Happy people refuse to use this ability to worry.

Some Results of Worry

If left unchecked, worry can lead to anxiety, cares, fear, tension, dread and other maladies.

Worry is a vicious attack of the enemy which can literally destroy a person's mind. It sends more people to the hospital with various sickness and disease than perhaps any other single cause. In many cases, it has produced mental disorders and nervous breakdowns.

How to Overcome Worry

God commands us in Romans 12:2 to not be conformed to this world, but to be transformed by the renewing of our mind. The word renew means to "up-date" your thinking. As you begin to renew your mind—to think differently—you will discover the truth of Proverbs 23:7: "For as he thinks within himself, so he is. . ."

The scripture in Ephesians 5:26 declares we are to wash our minds with the water of the Word. Therefore, we renew our mind by studying and meditating on God's Word.

The mind is a neutral faculty of the soul. What we actually think on is an act of the will. We can make two choices in regard to our mind.

1. What are the two choices? (Romans 8:6)
    a. _____
    b. _____
2. What is the result of each choice?
    a. _____
    b. _____

The word "death" means to separate. Physical death occurs when the spirit and soul separate from the body. The wages of sin is death, in that it separates you from God. Death also means to become weak, impotent, inactive, inoperative, to deprive of power.

When the mind is set upon circumstances, situations and problems instead of Jesus and the answer, the result will be to worry over what is going to happen.

For example, we all have had the experience of being faced with a misunderstanding between us and a loved one, friend, fellow worker, boss or neighbor. We must go to them and clear up the misunderstanding. First, we find the thought of talking to them creates unpleasant feelings. Next, we find ourselves trying to figure out exactly what we will say to them. Then we worry over how they will react and respond. In our imagination we will rehearse the conversation:

I'll say, "it really wasn't meant to hurt you, and I am sorry your feelings got hurt."

They will probably say, "well, if you were not so quick to react you would have seen it was not the way you thought." Then I will say, "yes, but you will have to admit that on the surface it appeared to be that way."

Then a horrible suggestion may surface: what if they will not receive me? Suppose they say, "I'd rather not discuss it with you, as it would only upset me all over again and right now I am able to control my feelings over the matter." Then I would say, ". . ." and on and on the warfare continues, thoughts flashing through our minds, up and down, back and forth. After awhile we try to stop the hassle, realizing it is foolish to keep this up, only to find that in a few minutes we are once again caught up in trying to figure out what to say.

Usually, when we get with the person it does not happen as we imagined. All our vain imagination produced was torment of the mind and emotions. It only served the purpose of our adversary to rob us of our peace of mind.

3. What is the first thing we must learn to do? (Phil. 4:8) _____

4. Who will tell you what to speak? (Matt. 10:19–20) _____

5. How must we respond to vain imagination, speculations and thoughts which are robbing us of our peace of mind? (II Cor. 10:3–5) _____

You cast down and destroy vain imaginations and speculations by disciplining yourself to keep your mind on Jesus.

Guard your thought life by placing your trust in God's ability to tell you what to say and how to say it.

Remember that although something may be true it may not be pure or lovely. Think only upon that which produces praise and thanksgiving.

For example, it may be true that the utility bill is so much more than expected you don't know how you can handle it. And, on top of that, you just received an unexpected insurance premium bill. To start worrying about paying the utility bill and imagining having your utilities turned off will rob you of your peace of mind.

Instead of letting your mind be captured by these thoughts, begin meditating and confessing God's Word:

Dan. 1:9: "Now God had brought Daniel into favor and tender love with the prince of the eunuchs."

Pr. 16:7 "When a man's way please the Lord He makes even his enemies be at peace with him."

Believe that you have favor with God and men. Think upon it. Meditate on the possibilities it creates. Confess that you have favor with others; they love you and you love them. Confess that God is working the problem out; that He is making peace.

Cast down and destroy the speculations and vain imaginations. Take the thoughts that exalt themselves against the Word of God and walk in victory.

Keeping your mind on Jesus means that you stand on the truths of the scripture and confess them instead of thoughts that oppose them.

Mal. 3:10–11 declares that a tithe causes God to pour out blessings on you and rebuke the devourer. If you have obeyed God's Word in giving and being a good steward of the money entrusted to you, expect God to keep His word.

Think upon those scriptures. Confess what God says about prosperity rather than the fear the devil will attempt to put upon you.

Phil 4:19 "My God shall supply all of my needs, according to His riches in glory in Christ Jesus.

Meditate upon it. Get it down into your spirit. Set your mind upon it. Believe it. Say it. Don't be robbed of your peace of mind. Instead of preparing for failure, begin to prepare for success. Stop dwelling on dire results and set your mind on God's answer. Be Jesus-centered, rather than problem-centered.

How to Overcome Anxiety

There are two powerful words the enemy constantly uses to put us at a disadvantage in the war of ideas and thoughts.

He capitalizes on our inability to know the beginning and end of our circumstances. He utilizes these two words to cause untold torment and harassment when we are facing an adverse situation.

These two powerful words are "WHAT IF?"
What if you get unexpected bills?
What if they never speak to you again?
What if you get sick and can't work?
What if you get laid off?
What if you can't handle it?
What if you backslide?
What if you can't pass the test?
What if your check-up reveals you have cancer?
What if those chest pains are a defective heart?
What if your customers stop buying your product?
I could go on. There is no end to the possibilities of "What If?"
The fact that we do not know the answers reveals our need for God. He knows the answers. He also knows how to direct our steps to make our end for good and not hurt.

6. What is the proper response to "What If?" (Phil. 4:6)

     a. _____

     b. _____

7. What is the result? (Phil. 4:7) _____

Discipline yourself to refuse anxiety over the "What If?" Instead of being anxious, begin to pray. Do as God commands. Don't be anxious over anything and pray about everything with an attitude of thanksgiving.

As you begin to do this the enemy may suggest you should not trouble God with your trivia. After all, God has so many important matters to consider you should leave Him alone.

The answer is simple: God Himself said to cast our cares on Him because He cares for us. He also told us to handle anxiety by praying about everything.

God is so interested in small details He numbered the hair on our heads; so we know He is interested in small details and everything that concerns us.

8. Jesus tells us in Luke 12:22–23 how to overcome anxiety:

    a. v. 22 What are we not to be anxious for? _____

    b. v. 23 What is life more than? _____

    c. v. 23 What is the body more than? _____

    d. v.24 Who feeds the birds? _____

    e. v. 24 Are you more valuable to God than birds? _____

    f. v. 25–26 What is a very little thing to God that man cannot do? _____

    g. v. 27–28 Who clothes the lilies and grass in the fields? _____

    h. 4. 28 Who will also clothe you? _____

    i. v. 29 What two things are you not to do?

      1. _____

      2. _____

    j. v. 30 Who eagerly seeks these things? _____

    k. v. 30 Who knows you need these things? _____

    l. v. 31 What are you to seek for? _____

    m. v. 31 What will be added to you? _____

    n. v. 32 Why should you not be afraid? _____

From these scriptures Jesus teaches us to overcome anxiety about food, drink, and clothing (i.e., our personal needs) by realizing the nature of our Father. As we look at the animal kingdom and vegetable kingdom we see they are cared for by our Father.

The lesson to be learned is that they just wait upon God for everything. The birds, the beasts, the insects are all cared for by God.

9. What does God give to cattle? (Ps. 104:14) _____

10. What does God give to the lions? (Ps. 104:21) _____

What the animal kingdom does by instinct, Jesus wants us to do intelligently, willingingly, and voluntarily. He admonishes us to realize we are more valuable than the animals. We are so valuable to God He died for us.

By choosing to be Jesus-centered instead of problem-centered you are on your way to victory, freedom from anxiety.

The Nature of Cares

In Mark, chapter four, Jesus tells a parable of the sower who went out to sow the Word. In verse fifteen He says satan will come immediately to take away the Word.

Therefore, we must constantly guard our hearts for we are in spiritual warfare and our enemy is quick to take advantage of every circumstance and situation.

One of the most effective ways of making the Word unfruitful, according to Mark 4:19, is the cares of this world and the deceitfulness of riches and the lust of things entering in.

The Greek word for cares is *merimna*, which means distraction, disunite. It is mental suffering, a troubling concern.

If you allow your mind to be distracted by the events, circumstances and situations of the world it will make the Word of God ineffective in your life.

How Cares Entangle Us

A good example of how cares are used in this warfare is found in Luke 10:38–42: "Now, as they were traveling along, He entered a certain village; and a woman named Martha welcomed Him into her home. And she had a sister called Mary, who moreover was listening to the Lord's Word, seated at His feet. But Martha was distracted with all her preparations; and she came up to Him and said, 'Lord, do You not care that my sister has left me to do all the serving alone? Then tell her to help me.' But the Lord answered and said to her, 'Martha, Martha, you are worried and bothered about so many things; but only a few things are necessary, really only one, for Mary has chosen the good part, which shall not be taken from her.' "

Martha asked the question that is on the heart of a lot of people: "Lord, do You not care?" It was the same question the disciples asked when their boat was in a storm and Jesus was sleeping. They awoke Him asking, "Lord, do you not care?"

The good news is that not only does Jesus care, He can do something about the cares.

11. What are we commanded to do with cares? (I Pet. 5:6–7) _____

From our study of Luke 12 on overcoming anxiety, recall that in verse thirty Jesus pointed out it was people of the world who sought things and had cares.

The Root Problem of Cares

I am firmly convinced that the root of any problem is the inability to trust God. We get our eyes off Jesus and onto the cares of the world. We can not see the solution. We forget that God cares and is able to handle the cares.

One reason why people do not trust God is very simple: they do not know Him. They may have some information and facts about God, but they do not know Him. They may have read the Bible, listened to tapes, heard sermons, and even talked about God; however, He is not real to them. This is revealed in the fact they do not trust Him.

12. Who puts their trust in God? (Ps. 9:10) _____

Those who know God will not be overcome with worry, anxiety and cares. They know that just as natural parents provide for their children, so will their Heavenly Father provide for them.

13. What has God promised those who trust Him?

    a. Pr. 28:25 _____

    b. Pr. 29:25 _____

    c. Ps. 25:20 _____

    d. Ps. 37:40

    1. _____

2. _____

3. _____

e. Ps. 5:12

1. _____

2. _____

f. I Chr. 5:19–22 _____

How to Overcome Cares

It does not cost to trust and obey God—it pays. God wants us to keep our mind on Him and hearts trusting in Him so that He can take care of our cares. He wants to be good to us. To bless us. He loves us. He cares for us. He will do for us according to His Word and produce in us freedom from care.

No wonder our enemy wants to distract us from the Word just as he did Martha. She was a hard worker, constantly busy serving Jesus and the other guests in her home. However, her sister Mary, recognizing an opportunity to learn from Jesus' teachings let the housework go and joined those listening to Jesus.

Martha was so busy she overlooked the important thing—the opportunity to learn from Jesus. She had her mind on the cares of preparation. It caused her to lose her peace. Instead of peace of mind she became anxious and frustrated. Not only was she upset with her sister, but she doubted if Jesus cared.

Jesus recognized her problem and gave her the solution: "only a few things are necessary, really only one, for Mary has chosen the good part, which shall not be taken from her."

So it will be with you and I. If we choose, as Mary, to keep our mind on Jesus we will find victory over cares. Instead of the Word being choked and becoming unfruitful it will grow, making us stronger and stronger. It will make us victorious over our enemies that war against the peace of our mind. It will give us that peace which passes understanding.

Questions to Stimulate Thought and Revelation from the Lord

14. What is worry? _____

15. What are some consequences of worry? _____

16. What two words are used to induce anxiety? _____

17. What is peace associated with in the scripture? _____

18. What must happen for our mind to enjoy peace? _____

19. How do you overcome worry, anxiety and cares? _____

20. How do you renew (update) your mind? _____

Answers to Questions

1. a. carnal minded
   b. spiritually minded
2. a. death
   b. life and peace
3. Guard thoughts
4. Holy Spirit
5. Cast down, destroy and take captive
6. Don't be anxious about anything, and pray about everything
7. Peace of God shall keep your hearts and minds
8. a. food and clothing
   b. meat
   c. clothing
   d. God
   e. yes
   f. cause growth
   g. God
   h. God
   i. 1. seek not what to eat or drink
      2. be not doubtful
   j. people of the world
   k. our Father
   l. the Kingdom of God
   m. all these things
   n. it is the Father's good pleasure to give us the Kingdom
9. Grass
10. Meat
11. Cast them upon the Lord
12. Those who know His name
13. a. will prosper
    b. will be exalted
    c. not be ashamed
    d. 1. He helps
       2. delivers from wicked
       3. saves
    e. 1. blessed
       2. surround him with favor as a shield
    f. victory over enemies and great spoils
14. To tease, trouble harass with importunity or with cares and anxiety
15. Anxiety, cares, fear, tension, and dread
16. What if
17. Trusting God
18. It must be renewed
19. Be Jesus-centered and not problem-centered
20. By making the choice to think differently—to focus our mind and thinking on God and His Word

CHAPTER TWELVE: NERVOUSNESS

Stress   Tension

Nervousness Defined

Whenever you think of a nervy person you think of someone strong and firm, as "that took a lot of nerve." However, when you think of nervousness the tendency is to think of a disorder of the nerves, being jittery or other nervous habits.

Evidence of Nervousness

The chart on page 80 shows "nervousness" as another weapon used by the enemy to steal our peace. That the enemy is successful is obvious by just looking around us. We have only to look at our fellow commuter on the bus or train or at work to see that we are living in an age of nervousness. It appears more and more people are being snared by the tension of our society.

Not only do we see it on their faces, but we are aware of many pill-poppers (drugs acting on the central nervous system exceed a billion dollars per year in sales), before-after-and in-between-dinner drinkers (just to calm the old nerves a bit), knuckle-crackers, touchy tempers, and those with their guts in a knot, others unable to sleep.

Doctors are aware of the problem due to their increased business. Industry is aware of the problem due to increased absenteeism, accidents, and alcoholism. Several programs have been initiated to help people adjust and overcome the vast number of emotional problems being created by environmental hazards—smog, traffic jams, noise and a hurried pace are taking their toll. Crime, drugs, inflation, energy crises, pollution, corruption all add to the burden. Over-demanding jobs, unhappy marriages, divorces, separations, wayward children and unfulfilled careers also take their toll. The list could go on to include the changing moral standards in society, increases in individual freedom and uncertain relationships with one another. It is easy to see why so many people are in bondage.

Because people are different in their personalities the ability to cope varies from one person to another. However, we all go through life trying to put up the best battle we can. It involves going forward, backwards, stepping aside or perhaps even running away. Then there are cycles of succeeding and failing.

Normal anxiety can be expected in all of us. Fleeting moments of fear when lightning begins to flash is normal. However, to be terrified and unable to go to sleep during a thunderstorm is not normal.

There are many events in life that also inflict stress upon us. Death of spouse, divorce, separation, death of a close family member, personal injury or illness, fired at work, retirement, pregnancy, change in work hours or conditions, change of residence or school and other natural occurring events in life can be used to launch a vicious attack on us mentally and emotionally by the enemy.

Children are also open to these attacks of the enemy. In fact, psychiatrists often say many cases of breakdowns as adults are connected to painful experiences of childhood. The central nervous system is least able to adapt during childhood when certain pressures are more acute in children than adults.

Stress will show up in children by thumb sucking, bedwetting or eating and sleeping problems. These can be brought on by a visit to a dentist, a new baby, tension between the parents or other family members, or entering kindergarten.

Some other examples of tension being expressed are teeth-gritting, lip-tightening or nail-biting. Other examples are becoming intensely angry at some small irritation, mistrust of friends and being suspicious of people, carrying a chip on the shoulder, finding it hard to sleep, being weary and tired with no explanation.

If tension becomes greater than our capacity to tolerate or cope with it, then the tension is channeled through the nervous system to body organs. It then may express itself as migraine headaches, ulcers, skin rashes, heart trouble, breathing problems such as asthma, high blood pressure, diabetes, arthritis, backache, loss of appetite and other maladies.

The wards of practically every psychiatric hospital have people lying about in them with their knees drawn up to their chest, back curved forward, lying as though they were in their mothers' womb; safe, warm and secure. They think they can shut out the world by keeping their eyes closed and covering their head.

Few drugs of today have caught on as those referred to as tranquilizers. This is partly because the word suggests "peace of mind." But in actuality, the word only refers to various "chemical crutches" that neither cure anything nor give "peace of mind."

Overcoming Nervousness

I recall receiving a phone call from a pastor who had a young man who was snared by nervousness and seemingly could not gain his freedom. The pastor asked if I would meet with him and the young man. We set up an appointment for them to come to my house. They arrived before I did and while visiting with my wife, waiting for me, a wreck occurred at the intersection by our house. They all went outside to help. I arrived just as the ambulance attendants were getting a young lady out of her car. She had cut her forehead, but did not appear to be seriously injured. The ambulance took her away.

We went back into the house where the pastor, the young man and I went into my study. The young man, whom I shall call Bill (not his real name), was in his mid-twenties, a school teacher, and loved Jesus. He had nice blond hair and blue eyes. He was single and lived in a Christian community house with other male Christians. He wa also co-pastor of his fellowship, along with the pastor who had contacted me.

He expressed gratitude for me seeing him and expressed trust that Jesus was going to use this occasion to set him free. In fact, he sensed the oppression of the enemy welling up within him as he was ministering to one of the persons involved in the accident. He told us how his heart had speeded up, his hands had trembled and that he had the sensation of

89

tension mounting within himself. He told me this type of attack had been plaguing him for years, but that he had trained himself not to let it manifest itself to others. However, it was getting worse and was hindering him in his relationship with Jesus. He had decided to expose it and obtain help. But before we could go on, he said he needed a few moments to collect himself.

I layed my hand on him and, in the name of Jesus, rebuked the nervousness and tension and spoke peace to his emotions. Immediately the peace of Jesus calmed him and released him from the oppression of the enemy.

It was interesting to listen as he related the various means the enemy used in bringing him into captivity to nervousness.

He had a very deep love for Jesus and desired to please Him. The enemy had taken advantage of this and continually pointed out how he did not please Jesus. he would be compelled to try harder and find that he still could not succeed. This created tension and put him under a tremendous strain.

He also wanted to be a good teacher. Again, the enemy took advantage of this and created pressure from his inabilities to always do everything right.

Fnally, the root of his problem emerged. As a young boy he had a domineering mother whom he could not please. As a result of this, he was constantly under the pressure and strain of trying to please her.

I had him pray and forgive his mother and to empty himself of resentment and bitterness toward her. After this we laid the axe to the root of his nervousness and ministered to him in the various areas of tension, nervous habits and physical problems brought on by his nervousness.

This is not an unusual story. Due to various factors, more and more people are seeking ways to relieve their nervousness and mental anguish. Thus we find a variety of programs being marketed and thousands of dollars being spent.

There is a very interesting story in the fourth chapter of Mark with regard to Jesus, "The Prince of Peace," getting into a ship and saying to His disciples, "Let us pass over unto the other side." He then went to the back of the ship and went to sleep. There arose a great storm. The winds and the waves beat onto the ship. The disciples awoke Jesus and said unto Him, "Do You not care if we perish?" He arose, and rebuked the wind, and said unto the sea, "Peace be still." And the wind ceased and there was great calm.

1. Why was Jesus able to lie down and sleep? (Psalm 4:8) _____

_____

As we go through life there will be storms from time to time. In the midst of these storms, we must turn our attention to Jesus, the Prince of Peace, who can calm the storm and give peace to us. We can not count on the peace of the world which tranquilizes the emotions for a period of time, either through drugs, booze, or mind control. We must instead look to the peace which passes all understanding.

2. How do we assure ourselves of being able to weather the storms of life? (Matt. 7:24–27) _____

_____

A sound relationship with Jesus Christ and a continuing in the Word will impart a confidence that is able to withstand the blowing winds and beating waves upon our house, because we know our house will not fall; its foundation is not build on sand but is build on a solid rock—Jesus Christ. We are assured that Jesus cares for us as shown by His death. He does not want us to perish in whatever storm we may find ourself caught in. On the contrary, he wants to bring us safely through it.

3. What does God say about man's peace? (Isaiah 59:8 & 48:22) _____
_____

4. What has God done about this?
   a. Isaiah 53:5 (KJ) _____
   b. Colossians 1:20 _____
   c. Romans 5:1 _____
   d. Luke 1:78–79 _____
5. Therefore, what should we do?
   a. II Tim. 2:22 _____
   b. Psalm 34:14 _____
   c. II Cor. 13:11 _____
6. What will be the result of seeking peace?
   a. Psalm 55:18 _____
   b. Psalm 29:11 _____
   c. Psalm 37:37 _____

Seek peace and pursue it. Seek, that is, the peace of God and not the peace of the world. There is no peace outside of God for He is the Prince of Peace. So it is folly to use the world's methods to overcome nervousness, tension and stress.

It is a fact that God wants us to live in peace. He provided the means in our Lord Jesus Christ. Everyone who has Jesus has peace. Therefore we are not seeking a thing called peace but a relationship with peace Himself that will deliver us from the adverse effects of the storms in our life. This is a peace that will set us free from habits and physical problems produced by nervousness. Keeping your mind on Jesus is not easy when the enemy is mounting his attack. Therefore we need to practice during the calm times in order to prevail when the storm comes.

How to Overcome Stress and Tension

I heard a testimony of a man who, as a young man, used to stutter while trying to talk. He also had the nervous habit of nail-biting. One day he became aware of the fact Jesus could heal him and give him peace. He began to believe that because of the Prince of Peace living inside he did not have to stammer or bite his nails. He began confessing this truth and soon found himself cured.

7. What is in the power of the tongue? (Proverbs 18:21) _____
8. How can you control your mind and body? (James 3:2–5) _____
_____
9. What will be the result? (Proverbs 13:3) _____
10. What do counselors of peace have? (Proverbs 12:20) _____
11. How do you make a heart glad? (Proverbs 12:25) _____
12. What is a soothing tongue? (Proverbs 15:4) _____
13. What did Jesus teach about our words in Mark 11:23? _____
_____

I read somewhere that about 85% of all illnesses were psychosomatic and not organic. In other words, the problems were induced by emotional factors.

Medical science tells us the speech center controls the central nervous system. In so doing they are agreeing with the Word of God. If we also agree with God's Word and begin to confess it as truth the impact upon our nervous system will be health and life. Our minds will be "renewed" or "updated." Our cares will be cast upon the Prince of Peace. Our minds will be trained to be on Jesus who is our peace. The result will be freedom from nervousness and its symptoms.

Questions to Stimulate Thought and Revelation from the Lord

14. Why are some people able to cope with circumstances better than others? _____

15. What are some stress factors which give you a problem? _____

16. What are tranquilizers? _____

17. What do they do? _____
18. Who is able to give "peace of mind?" _____
19. How is it possible to break nervous habits? _____
20. How is tension released? _____
21. What may be the result? _____
22. How can you be free from nervousness? _____

23. If you have been plagued by nervousness, tension, stress and nervous habits, begin this moment to gain victory by saying this or a similar prayer:

"Father, Your Word says to come boldly to the throne of grace to obtain mercy and find grace in time of need. Lord you know every need I have in my physical body. You know every need I have in my mind and emotions. You know every need I have in my family circle. You know every heartache I have. Father, I have made wrong confessions and have said wrong things that have brought the things that are destructive upon my life. I ask you to forgive me and in the name of Jesus I break the power, dominion and influence of those words and confessions. I now make a new confession based upon Your Word; You cause me to dwell in safety, therefore I am not afraid of the circumstances. I am strong and of good courage. I am not afraid of life nor death. I am not dismayed because You are with me wherever I go. You are the strength of my life. You are directing my steps. You are going to hear me say whenever someone asks how are you, "Well, the Lord is my Shepherd and I do not have a care. I am blessed of the Lord and whatsoever I do shall prosper." I will have a good report for all who meet me. I will not talk of ill health, sickness, or problems, but I will talk as one blessed of the Lord. Father, I praise and thank You that these words are true and I have whatsoever I say." Amen.

Answers to Questions

1. He knew God made him to dwell in safety
2. Building our lives on the Word of God
3. They know not the way of peace and have no peace
4.
   a. the chastisement of our peace was upon Him
   b. made peace through the blood of His cross
   c. we have peace with God through our Lord Jesus Christ
   d. He guides our feet into the way of peace
5.
   a. follow after peace
   b. seek and pursue peace
   c. live in peace
6.
   a. soul will be delivered
   b. strength and blessing
   c. perfect and upright
7. Life and death
8. With your tongue
9. Keep your life (soul)
10. Joy
11. Good word
12. Tree of life
13. Have what you say
14. Difference in personality
15. No right or wrong answer for this one
16. Chemical crutches
17. They neither cure or give peace of mind
18. The Prince of Peace
19. Keeping your mind on Jesus
20. Through the nervous system to body organs
21. Migraine headaches, ulcers, skin rashes, heart trouble, breathing problems, high blood pressure, diabetes, arthritis, backache, loss of appetite
22. Agree with God's Word and begin to confess it as truth

CHAPTER THIRTEEN: DREAD

Distress   Terror

Dread Defined

Another weapon the enemy uses to steal our peace is dread: uneasiness or alarm, excited by expected pain, loss or other evil; it is great fear or apprehension of evil or danger.

Results of Dread

Not only does dread rob you of your peace of mind, it creates vivid images of impending disaster or misfortune. If left unchecked, this can produce terror and distress which can paralyze or immobilize you in various situations. Instead of being on the offense and winning the spiritual warfare you are unable to cope with your circumstances.

Causes of Dread

We are all vulnerable to the attack of dread due to our inability to see and foretell the future. Therefore, unexpected events and circumstances are used to inflict dread upon unsuspecting victims.

For many people, all unknown events are going to end in some type of disaster, misfortune or evil. Depending upon the degree of captivity, it may produce mild forms of apprehension to paralyzing terror. This is not to indicate you are taken captive because you experience some kind of emotional response whenever you are about to speak before an audience, meet a stranger, go for a job interview, or other similar events. There is a distinct difference in having an emotional response, which is quite normal, than the bondage of dread, terror and distress that agitate the body and mind.

1. What is the reason for dread coming upon a person? (Pro. 1:20–29) _____

_____

Our enemy is a big bully who makes false claims as to his power. He is not God, nor is he the opposite of God. He is a created being. An angel that rebelled against God and consequently was cast out of the kingdom of God. He has not, nor will he ever, defeat God. In fact, our God knows no defeat. If you don't know this and, therefore, ignore the voice of God, it will cost you dearly. Dread will stalk you continuously.

For example, your boss says he wants to see you in his office immediately. You begin to wonder what is going on. Your mind races over recent events, and hears the suggestion, "he's going to fire me. Why? I don't know why, but I must have done something wrong, otherwise he would not want to see me immediately."

Dread begins to come upon you. "Even if he doesn't fire me, he is going to chew me out for something I've done wrong. If only I knew what it was, I could have a good explanation ready." Soon, you're in a cold sweat. Your imagination is running wild. The result is a loss of your peace of mind. You begin to feel sick, nauseated. Your nerves are on edge. The stress is becoming unbearable. You would rather do anything than go into his office. Finally, you muster up the courage to go into his office. You search his face for a clue as to how he is feeling. Your eyes dart down to his desk. Perhaps there is a piece of paper with a clue as to what he is up to. As he begins to speak you tense up, straining to catch the tone of his voice as this will indicate his mood.

He asks some simple questions about a job you are doing. You give him the answers and leave his office. He didn't fire you, was not mad or upset. What a relief. You begin to relax and feel foolish for getting uptight. You can't imagine why you thought he would be firing you. Why, just the other day he complimented you on getting a report out ahead of schedule. Suddenly, it's a beautiful day. Everything is going great.

Overcoming Dread

A higher, better way of living is to be free from this type of bondage by learning how to keep our mind on Jesus and trusting in Him.

While it is true we can not foretell the future and will face unexpected events, such as the one described, it is also true that God is for us and not against us.

God delights in His children; it gives Him pleasure to deliver us from our enemies. Whenever dread attempts to come upon us, we need only to cry out to God and run into our fortress and high tower for safety. *Our enemies can not pursue us into the presence of God.* As we draw nigh to God, He strengthens us so that we can resist the enemy and make him flee from us. As we grow stronger, the time will come when we will pursue our enemies until we catch them and utterly destroy them and make them as ashes under our feet.

2. Why has God prepared a throne room? (Heb. 4:14–16) _____
3. What is the result of listening to God? (Pro. 1:33) _____
4. What does God always cause us to do? (II Cor. 2:14) _____
5. How did David overcome dread? (Psalm 27:1) _____

Overcoming Distress

Distress is the result of believing or fearing that some type of sickness, calamity or misery of some kind is going to come upon you.

I remember reading an article one time about a man who lost ten million dollars on the stock market and became so distressed he jumped out a window and committed suicide. To my amazement, the article concluded by stating he still had thirty million dollars. There is no way of knowing what terrible pictures were in his mind as he pondered his stock losses.

6. What did Jesus say would happen before He returns? (Luke 21:25–26)
   a. _____
   b. _____
   c. _____

7. What are we to do? (Luke 21:28)
   a. _____
   b. _____
8. Why? _____

Whatever you may be facing in life at this very moment does not mean it can not be changed or that it is going to result in some type of calamity. It may be proof that time is running out for our enemy and that Jesus is nigh to returning. Remember that the things of this world are indeed passing away. But the Kingdom of God is increasing and shall never pass away. Therefore, keep your eyes on Jesus and not on the things of this world.

The apostle Paul had many opportunities to be overcome by the enemy, as he shares in his letters to the Corinthians.

In II Corinthians 1:8 he tells of facing so much trouble in Asia that he and his team despaired even of life. I would paraphrase this as he was feeling so bad he wasn't even sure if dying would make him feel better. Yet, he didn't go under; he was not defeated. In chapter four he gives us the answer as to how he was able to win in his own spiritual warfare.

9. Why would Paul not look at things seen? (II Cor. 4:18) _____
   _____
10. What are things unseen? (II Cor. 4:18) _____
11. What are the results of looking at things unseen? (II Cor. 4:16–17)
    a. _____
    b. _____
    c. _____
12. How is another way to find help in time of trouble? (I Thess. 3:7) _____
    _____
13. What can one and two people do? (Deut. 32:30) _____
14. What happens if three band together? (Ecc. 4:12) _____

Overcoming Terror

Terror is different from dread in that it comes suddenly upon you. It is extreme fear and fright that agitates the body and mind. It is violent dread. There are many instances in the scriptures of terror coming upon individuals and whole armies. Reference is made to the terror of God coming upon the wicked. It is a terrible thing to fall into the hands of a living God—if you are not right with Him.

The disciples were overcome by terror when faced with a sudden storm on the sea of Galilee. They thought they were going to perish and awoke Jesus out of His sleep and cried out, "Master, do you not care that we perish?" (Mark 4:35–41)

Peter warns us in I Pet. 3:14 that threatenings of wicked men or evil apprehended from them can cause terror to come upon us and tells us to not be afraid of their terror, neither be troubled.

15. What had caused terror to come upon David? (Psalm 55:3–5)
    a. _____
    b. _____
16. What type of terror did it produce? (Psalm 55:4) _____

17. What did it make David think of doing? (Psalm 55:6) _____
18. What did David do to win the war? (Psalm 55:16–17)

    v. 16 _____

    v. 17

    a. _____

    b. _____

19. How often would David do this? (Psalm 55:17) _____
20. What was the result? (Psalm 55:18) _____

Through learning to keep our mind on Jesus, and thus releasing peace, we discover that the test and trials of today can be overcome. Instead of yielding to the voice of the enemy that we shall perish, we place our trust in God. We call out to Him day and night and He delivers us. What do we cry out? We cry out what God says in His Word:

"The Lord is my light and my salvation; whom shall I fear? The Lord is the strength of my life; of whom shall I be afraid?

I am strong in the Lord and in the power of His might. Therefore, I command dread, terror and distress to leave me. I command weakness out of my body.

I have power over all power of the enemy and nothing shall by any means hurt me. I can do all things through Jesus Christ who strengthens me. I will not dread the task before me because Jesus is my strength and wisdom. (Psalm 27:1; Luke 10:19; Philippians 4:13)

You could also take Psalm 91 and make it your confession, declaring it to be true for your life.

Questions to Stimulate Thought and Revelation from the Lord

21. How do many people see unknown events ending? _____
22. What is the difference between a normal emotional response and an attack by the enemy? _____
23. How do we aid dread coming upon us? _____
24. How can we win the battle? _____
25. If you have been snared by dread, pray this prayer or one similar to it:

Father, forgive me for not trusting you and casting down vain imaginations of impending evil, calamities and misery. I now take the authority you have given me over all power of the enemy in the Name of Jesus and command _____
(dread, terror, distress) to flee from me. I beak its power, dominion and influence in my life and declare that Jesus is my light and my salvation. That Jesus is my strength and life. Thank you Jesus for delivering me from all alarm. Amen.

Answers to Questions

1. Refusing to listen and obey the voice of wisdom

2. That we may find grace to help in time of need

3. Dwell safely and quietly from fear of evil

4. To triumph in Christ

5. He trusted God to be his light, salvation and defense

6. a. there shall be signs in heaven
   b. distress upon the earth
   c. the powers of heaven shall be shaken

7. a. look up
   b. lift up your heads

8. Because our redemption draws nigh

9. Because they are temporal

10. Eternal

11. a. we faint not
    b. inward man is renewed
    c. works for us a far more exceeding and eternal weight of glory

12. Through the faith of others

13. One can put a thousand to flight and two ten thousand

14. A threefold cord is not easily broken

15. a. voice of the enemy
    b. oppression of the wocked

16. Death

17. Fly away like a dove

18. v. 16 call upon God
    v. 17
    a. pray
    b. cry aloud

19. Evening and morning

20. He delivered his soul in peace

21. In disaster

22. An attack by the enemy robs us of our peace of mind, while a normal emotional response does not bring us into the bondage of dread, distress and terror

23. By yielding to vain imaginations

24. To think positive, draw near to God and resist the enemy